D1362430

THE
ROTTWEILER

Centuries of Service

LINDA MICHELS AND CATHERINE THOMPSON

HOWELL BOOK HOUSE
NEW YORK

Howell Book House
A Simon & Schuster Macmillan Company
1633 Broadway
New York, NY 10019-6785

Macmillan Publishing books may be purchased for business or sales promotional use. For information please write: Special Markets Department, Macmillan Publishing USA, 1633 Broadway, New York, NY 10019-6785.

MACMILLAN is a registered trademark of Macmillan, Inc.
ISBN 0-87605084-4
Cataloging-in-Publication data available upon request from the Library of Congress

Manufactured in the United States of America
10 9 8 7 6 5 4 3 2

Cover and book design by George J. McKeon

Dedication

We dedicate this book to our Rottweilers past, present and future. After all, it was and is our Rottweilers who fill our lives and give us the information to write this book. We will not name names because all of our dogs have held and hold a place near and dear to our hearts. Some achieved greater success than others, some had long lives, others very short ones, but all were important to our education in Rottweilers.

They gave unquestioning loyalty and devotion. They saved us from dangerous situations, listened to our sad tales of woe and brought smiles to our faces. They taught us humility. They taught us perseverance. They gave us great highs when successful and tore out our hearts when they were sick or had to be put down. For all these reasons and some we did not say, this book is for them.

Acknowledgments

I must thank my husband, Greg, who has allowed and encouraged my involvement with Rottweilers. Without his constant urging, common sense and devotion I would not have taken on this project.

I would also like to thank Hermann Heid, who entrusted me with my first Rottweiler, and Felice Luburich, who has mentored me through the years, graciously sharing her knowledge of the breed and dogs in general. —*Cathy Thompson*

First and foremost, I thank my husband, Bill, who has shared my love for Rottweilers and who has unselfishly allowed me to take most of the credit for the success of our breeding program and knowledge of Rottweilers and dogs in general. He has supported me through this project without complaint.

I thank Jane Justice for her help and ideas with this book. She has researched and supplied me with many topics for these chapters. She has also been a great friend and mentor over the past ten years. She is a commonsense dog woman on whom I often rely for sound advice. The Rottweiler is very lucky to have Jane.

Sue Suwinski introduced me to Rottweilers and is responsible for laying the foundation for my thirst for knowledge of dog behavior, structure and realism in breeding dogs. She taught me that considering beauty only is a disservice to any breed. I thank her for her generosity of knowledge and patience with a novice who phoned her almost every day for five years. I thank her for giving me a lifetime of enjoyment with Rottweilers. She is ultimately responsible for my being able to write this book.

Lastly, I thank all of the "dog people" in the Finger Lakes Kennel Club and Ithaca Dog Training Club who have known me longer than I have owned Rottweilers. I was a member of both clubs for two years when my son died in 1978. My "non-doggy" friends stayed away, afraid of saying something wrong; the dog people dragged me to lunch, dog training and dog shows for months. They are responsible for my sanity. —*Linda Michels*

There are many more people who have taught us so much about Rottweilers and dogs in general. You may not even know who you are, but we thank you, too, for making this book possible.

Contents

Introduction   xiii

1. PROFILE OF THE ROTTWEILER   1

King of His Domain 1 • Things You Should Know 2

2. HISTORY OF THE ROTTWEILER   5

The Evolution of the Rottweiler 6 • How the Rottweiler Got His Name 7 • The Rottweiler's Neighbors 8 • Clubs for the Breed 9 • Establishing the Breed in the U.S. 10 • Early Champions 10 • From Not to Hot 11 • Famous Owners 13

3. OFFICIAL STANDARD OF THE ROTTWEILER   15

The AKC Standard of the American Rottweiler 17 • General Appearance 17 • Size, Proportion, Substance 17 • Head 18 • Ears 18 • Neck, Topline, Substance 19 • Forequarters 20 • Hindquarters 21 • Coat 21 • Color 22 • Gait 23 • Temperament 24 • Disqualifications 27

4. FINDING THE RIGHT DOG—PUPPY, ADULT OR RESCUE   29

*Think Health First 30 • Expect Questions 31 • The Sales Contract 32 •
The Pedigree 33 • Registration Papers 34 • Rottweiler Rescue 35 •
Boy or Girl? 35*

5. LIVING WITH A ROTTWEILER   39

*A Close Companion 40 • Helpful Handling 42 • Rottweilers and
Children 43 • Your Big Dog 45 • Toys and Games 45 • Equipment
You'll Need for Your Dog 47 • Your Rottweiler's Adolescence 48 •
Desexing Your Rottweiler 51*

6. KEEPING YOUR ROTTWEILER HAPPY AND HEALTHY   53

*Your Dog's Diet 53 • Crates 54 • Veterinary Care 56 •
Fleas 57 • Ticks 58 • Common Health Concerns 58 • Health
Red Flags 66*

7. CARING FOR YOUR ROTTWEILER   69

Rottweiler Essentials 70

8. GROOMING YOUR ROTTWEILER   73

Teeth and Nails 74 • Bathing Your Dog 76

9. SHOWING YOUR ROTTWEILER   79

*Learning to Show 80 • Entering a Show 81 • The Big Show 82 •
Your Turn in the Ring 84 • Professional Handlers 86 • Bear in
Mind 89*

10. OBEDIENCE TRIALS, PERFORMANCE EVENTS AND   91
    OTHER ACTIVITIES FOR YOUR ROTTWEILER

    Obedience 92 • Tracking 94 • Agility 95 • Herding 96 •
    Other Fun Events 97 • Therapy Work 98 • Schutzhund 98 •
    Search and Rescue 101

11. HEADLINERS   103

    Rottweiler Firsts 105

12. WHAT YOU SHOULD KNOW ABOUT BREEDING   111

    Evaluating Your Rottweiler 112 • Evaluating Yourself 113 • Why
    Breed? 115 • If You Think You're Ready 117 • The Male 117 •
    The Stud Contract 119 • Bring in the Bitch 121 • The Mating 123 •
    The Bitch 127 • Bitches and Puppies 128 • Risks and Rewards 129

13. SPECIAL CARE FOR THE OLDER ROTTWEILER   133

    The Aging Process 133 • Signs of Old Age 134 • Nutrition 135 •
    Exercise 137 • Grooming 138 • Introducing Another Pet 139 •
    When the Time Comes 140

14. THE AMERICAN ROTTWEILER CLUB   145

    ARC Specialty Shows 146 • Not Just Show Dogs 148

    EPILOGUE   151

    APPENDIX A   Organizations and Other Resources   153

    APPENDIX B   The American Rottweiler Club
    Mandatory Practices   157

APPENDIX C   The Meaning of All Those Titles   161

APPENDIX D   The Hall of Fame: American
Rottweiler Club Production Awards   167

APPENDIX E   Specialty Winners   175

APPENDIX F   The Thompson wHELPing Box   181

Bibliography   184

Index   187

(Thompson)

Introduction

After Cathy's nearly thirty years and Linda's twenty-one years of sharing our lives with Rottweilers, having the chance to write about them gives us the opportunity to give back to this marvelous breed a little of the love our dogs have given to us. This book also gives us the chance to pass on to others the practical knowledge and insight given us by our wonderful mentors.

We both have shown and trained Rottweilers in conformation, obedience and almost all performance events. We have also gained a wealth of knowledge from one of the most difficult of all dog-related volunteer jobs—we have taught household obedience classes. It is amazing how much you can learn about your own breed by teaching novice owners to train their unruly adult dogs. Through our hands-on experiences, we try to give sound advice to educate Rottweiler owners on the correct character, temperament and care of the breed.

It is our hope that this book will help all Rottweilers to find the proper homes, and all owners to find the proper Rottweilers—matches that will bring immeasurable joy to both dogs and owners.

Both authors have been very active in national and local Rottweiler, all-breed and obedience clubs. We have both held about every position in a dog club, from cleanup to show chairman at dog shows and gopher to president at club meetings. We have served on or chaired just about every committee, too, which has helped immensely in authoring this book. We are grateful for all our experiences and challenges.

Linda P. Michels has been active in the sport of dogs since 1976 and with Rottweilers since 1978. She has bred Rottweilers using the kennel name Lindenwood. She has trained and shown Rottweilers in conformation, obedience, tracking, Schutzhund and flyball, and was a Chief Tester for the American Temperament Society. She has also shown and attempted to train Samoyeds, a Siberian Husky, a Pug and a Smooth Fox Terrier.

Catherine M. Thompson has been active with Rottweilers since the late 1960s. She has bred Rottweilers using the kennel name Von Gailingen. She is an approved American Kennel Club judge of the breed as well as all obedience classes. She has judged Rottweiler specialties all over the U.S. and Canada, as well as countries like New Zealand, Australia, Jamaica, Trinidad and the Philippines. She was the first breeder/owner of an AKC Champion-Utility Dog Tracker titled Rottweiler.

(Donna and Karl Rice)

CHAPTER 1

Profile of the Rottweiler

No one really wants a big, black, mean dog who eats people. Unfortunately, this is the public perception of the Rottweiler today, but is it true? This is certainly not the original function for the breed, nor is it what Rottweiler breeders and fanciers think of these noble dogs. Can it happen? Of course! With poor training, lack of socialization and ignorant owners, the Rottweiler, with its power and strength, can wreak havoc in neighborhoods. But with training, socialization and responsible owners, the Rottweiler is a wonder dog—it's up to you to make the difference.

Most people are attracted to the Rottweiler because of his compact, muscular build, short coat and large head. His black-and-mahogany coloring is quite appealing. His athletic abilities are quite surprising. It is his temperament that is misunderstood.

The Rottweiler has strong instincts to protect his home and family. He is strong, loyal and powerful, yet he can be gentle and playful with his family. He is aloof with strangers but is persistent and insistent that his family pet him or throw a ball for him to retrieve. He is ready for whatever comes his way.

KING OF HIS DOMAIN

The Rottweiler is a breed of dog who, for centuries, has served mankind in numerous ways. He is an excellent guard, herding, tracking and companion animal. He is loyal and devoted to his human family. He is calm and confident in his environment. He is also independent, willful, bossy and wants to make all

The Rottweiler is an athletic dog whose muscular build and black-and-mahogany coloring appeal to many people. (G. A. J. Kuijpers)

do not have the time, patience and strength of character to own a Rottweiler, there are plenty of other breeds.

Because the Rottweiler has a reasonably short coat, his grooming needs are minimal. Brushing a Rottweiler when he is blowing coat is highly recommended, and an occasional bath, regular nail trimming and attention to clean teeth is all that is really required. The Rottweiler does have a double coat, so it is quite thick and dense. Rottweiler hair does get in the sugar bowl and butter dish, so neat freaks be forewarned.

THINGS YOU SHOULD KNOW

The Rottweiler is in the Working or Utility classification of dog breeds. He is considered medium large, but because of his heavy bone and musculature, he is heavier than other breeds of the same height. Just because he is relatively heavy does not mean that he is slow and lazy. Rottweilers require some daily exercise both mentally and physically. If not, they will devise their own entertainment, which is usually not in the best interest of their surroundings. Digging, barking and chewing are just a few naughty behaviors that come to mind when thinking of a bored Rottweiler.

Unfortunately, neighbors and homeowners' insurance companies have confused irresponsible Rottweiler owners with the temperament of a great breed. Many insurance companies have canceled homeowners' insurance policies, even

the decisions. He can and will share his home with other animals but prefers to act alone as king of his domain.

It is this bossiness, this king-of-the-yard attitude, that can and does get the Rottweiler into trouble. Ignorant owners do not seem to understand that large, independent-thinking dogs need training, socialization and attention. When treated with respect, fairness and consistency, he is easily trained.

This is not a breed that does well unattended. Rottweilers need to be part of their human family, and they must know their place in the family hierarchy.

For those of us who have come to know and love this breed, there is no other. For those who

Rottweilers want and need to be part of a family. (Beenen)

little too rough. The Rottweiler requires a fenced yard, must be kept under control at all times and must be allowed to run loose only in the safest of environments.

If you want a loyal companion who is moderately active, quite intelligent, not too much work to groom and is on the large side, perhaps a Rottweiler is for you. If you want a dog who can and will bring a smile to your face, protect you when needed and listen to your sad tales of woe, perhaps a Rottweiler is for you. If you want a dog who will never let you out of his sight around the house, perhaps a Rottweiler is for you. If you have the time, the energy and the will to mold a good canine citizen, then perhaps a Rottweiler is for you.

those of long standing with no claims, simply because a Rottweiler lives in the house. Many neighbors are extremely frightened and will call the local authorities if a Rottweiler steps out of the house. Rottweiler ownership is a huge responsibility.

Responsible Rottweiler ownership means keeping your Rottweiler safe and keeping anyone or anything the dog comes into contact with safe as well. A properly socialized Rottweiler is a pleasure to be around. Your relatives, friends and neighbors will enjoy being around your dog. They may actually like visiting your house. Lead by example: Educate the public with a properly trained, socialized dog who is never allowed to roam the streets or to be tied or chained in the yard. He must never be left unattended with children because he is large and may knock them down or play a

Because they are heavy bodied, muscular dogs, some people are afraid of Rottweilers. That's why owning one is a big responsibility. (Thompson)

CHAPTER 2

History of the Rottweiler

Our Friend the Rottweiler

- *the war dog of the ancient Roman legions*

- *the dog of butchers and cattle dealers in the Middle Ages*

- *the modern working dog at the service of institutions and the sport of dogs.*

—Our Friend the Rottweiler, *J.A.U. Yrüolüa and Elvi Tikka, translated from Finnish, Powderhorn Press, Hollywood, CA*

This quote is the history of the Rottweiler in a nutshell. It describes the Rottweiler's heritage as a working-class dog, not a dog pampered by the upper class or royalty. The Rottweiler of today was created by centuries of dogs who had to earn their keep. In a sense, they were developed to be the "blue-collar workers" of Europe.

How did the Rottweiler develop from ancient times to today's rank as the second-most-popular dog registered by the American Kennel Club? The history of Europe had a lot to do with the creation of the dog we know as the Rottweiler. The habits of man also play an important part. To fully answer the opening question of this paragraph, we will start with ancient history, which will help paint a picture of traits that have molded the modern Rottweiler.

THE EVOLUTION OF THE ROTTWEILER

During the Bronze Age, man left his gathering and hunting ways behind and began to settle in one place. He also started to keep flocks of sheep and herds of cattle for food and clothing needs. Man needed rather large dogs to protect these animals from predators and, of course, other humans. In ancient Rome, these dogs were known as the Mollosus.

The Mollossers were large dogs, and their existence has been documented to before the birth of Christ. Their history traces to the Tibetan Mastiff and other dogs of western Asia that were brought back to Rome with traders and armies. In fact, many breeds of stock guardians like the Rottweiler can be traced back through the Mollosus to the Tibetan Mastiff. Breeds such as the Great Pyrenees, Komondor, Marema, Kuvasz and Anatolian readily show this heritage. Although they share a common ancestry, the breeds developed differently according to the needs of man in the various regions of Europe where the dogs lived.

To the Rottweiler goes considerable credit for helping change the map and races of Europe. Of course, the Rottweiler's part in these changes was purely involuntary; nevertheless, if it had not been for him, the Roman armies would not have been able to negotiate the mighty Alps and pour down into central Europe.

—The Complete Dog Book, *1964, The American Kennel Club, Garden City Books, Garden City, NY*

The Rottweiler earned his place at man's side in part for his ability to protect flocks of sheep, something he still does to this day. (Debbie Eckles)

This quote certainly gives the Rottweiler a lot of credit for shaping history. But how did he and the other Mollosser breeds get to Europe from Rome? During the Roman campaigns in Europe (like Caesar's invasion of Britain in 54 and 50 B.C., the conquest of Gaul, circa 55 B.C., and the attack on Germany, circa 70 A.D.), traders and armies marched north from the Mediterranean through the Alps and from Britain south, bringing dogs of war that undoubtedly mixed with the local dogs used as stock guardians.

A German Champion-level Rottweiler of the 1950s.

HOW THE ROTTWEILER GOT HIS NAME

Because the major paths of travel followed alpine passes and rivers, trading centers and cities formed along them. One such South German city founded by the Romans on the Neckar River became known as *Rottweil* for its red-tiled roofs. Because Rottweil was a trading center, perhaps even a quartermaster depot for the Roman Army, there were many butchers in the area. During the Middle Ages, the dogs that accompanied the butchers became known as *Rottweil Butcher's dogs* and today are known as *Rottweilers.*

> *"Butcher's Dog of Rottweil" was the name he earned in a thriving market center in Wurttemberg. Livestock dealers setting out to buy cattle in the countryside thwarted thieves by tying their purses around his muscular neck; later he would drive their new bought herds back to market. Merchants harnessed the sturdy dogs to carts and posted him as guard.*
>
> *—Man's Best Friend National Geographic Book of Dogs, Melville Bell Grosvenor, 1958, 1966 National Geographic Society*

Were there enough butchers in Rottweil to develop a breed of dog? History does not leave enough records to verify that fact, nor does the lore of the money purses around the dogs' necks. What is, perhaps, more plausible, is that the butchers, on their buying trips, visited local farmers. When the butchers saw the usefulness of the farm dogs, they traded for or purchased pups.

What kind of dog did the farmers have? Economics of the era would demand a very versatile animal, one that could courageously guard the

German farmers who developed the Rottweiler needed a courageous, versatile dog to assist and protect them and their livestock. (Thompson)

farmer, his family and his livestock. One that could pull loads to market. One that could also help bring in the flocks and herds. One that possessed an undercoat to protect it from the damp cold. This is also the kind of dog that was useful to the local Rottweil butchers.

THE ROTTWEILER'S NEIGHBORS

Over the years, the city of Rottweil had many ties with Switzerland. It either sided with the Swiss in wars and battles or signed treaties of neutrality. In Switzerland, four breeds of farm dogs known as *Sennenhund* were developed. They are now known as the *Greater Swiss Mountain Dog,* the *Bernese Mountain Dog,* the *Entlebucher* and the *Appenzeller.* It is theorized that the foundations of these four breeds and that of the Rottweiler followed the same tracks. All five breeds had similar jobs. Because the cattlemen of Rottweil traveled into Switzerland to trade, it is easy to understand that interbreeding between these five breeds could have, and did, happen. The Swiss breeds are thought to have remained more pure because of their geographic isolation, whereas the Rottweiler, because of living in the midst of a trade route, was probably also crossed with outside breeds used for fighting and hunting wild boar.

With the outside infusion of fighting and hunting dogs, the Rottweiler became an even stronger guardian. When the Rottweiler lost his main job as the butcher's dog with the advent of railroads to take cattle to market and the banning of dogs used as draft animals, he was strong enough in character and temperament to take on other chores, such as

In these old photos of a Bernese Mountain Dog (top) and a Rottweiler, you can see how they may have descended from the same stock.

police and protection work. In fact, legend claims there was only one Rottweiler left in Rottweil in 1905. We're glad his character and working ability had won favor with farmers and butchers outside the town of Rottweil, or the breed would have become extinct.

At the turn of the 20th century, the Rottweiler was described in various forms of literature. Also, crosses to other than the Swiss Sennenhunds (all tricolored breeds) could be seen, because the Rottweiler was said to be black and yellow, yellow with black spots, yellow with black mask and ash gray with black spots and yellow markings.

When industry made the Rottweiler's job as the butcher's dog obsolete, he became valued more for his strong protective instincts. (R. & D. Wayburn)

CLUBS FOR THE BREED

From the late 1800s until 1920, there were many Rottweiler clubs in Germany that kept stud books and worked toward standards of Rottweiler type. In 1920 the various Rottweiler clubs agreed to join as one, and in 1921 the *Allgemeiner Deutscher Rottweiler Klub* (ADRK) was formed, which is still the governing Rottweiler club of Germany today.

In 1924 the ADRK published its first Rottweiler standard, which stated that the Rottweiler was black and tan. The other colors were no longer recognized because dogs that were other than black with tan were suspected to be of mixed breeding.

The first known Rottweilers in the United States were brought over by German immigrants who settled on the East Coast in 1928. These Germans were also members of the ADRK, and the first recorded litter of Rottweilers in the United States was whelped by one of their bitches, Zilly v.d. Steinlach, in 1930. Since the Rottweiler was not recognized by the American Kennel Club yet, this litter was recorded by the German Stud Book of the ADRK.

The first Rottweiler registered by the AKC was Stina vom Felsenmeer in 1931, even though there was no AKC standard for the Rottweiler. She was owned by August Knecht, one of the German immigrants/ADRK members who came over in 1928. The first American Kennel Club–registered litter was born in 1931 to Stina, and it was known

The Rottweiler was officially recognized by the American Kennel Club in 1935. This is CH Anka Von Gailingen, an American Rottweiler Club Gold Dam owned and bred by Catherine Thompson.

were, however, three rather strong local clubs (The Colonial Rottweiler Club on the East Coast, the Medallion Rottweiler Club in the Midwest and the Golden State Rottweiler Club in California) that tried to maintain the breed and educate others about it. In the early '70s, another attempt was made, and in 1973 the American Rottweiler Club, Inc. was founded. It held its first National Specialty in 1981; it became a member club of the American Kennel Club in 1991 with Mrs. Bernard Freeman named as its delegate. The *American Rottweiler Club* (ARC) revised the standard of the breed in 1979 and again in 1990.

EARLY CHAMPIONS

The first AKC-titled Rottweiler was Gero v. Rabenhorst, owned and trained by Arthur Alfred Eichler of Wisconsin. He earned his Companion Dog title (CD) in 1939, his Companion Dog Excellent title (CDX) in 1940 and his Utility Dog title (UD) in 1941. It took 27 years for a second Rottweiler to earn a UD.

as the "A" of Wellwood litter. This litter was also registered with the ADRK. The AKC officially recognized the Rottweiler in 1935 with the publishing of the first American standard.

ESTABLISHING THE BREED IN THE U.S.

An attempt to found a national Rottweiler club failed in the '60s. There

Mrs. Bernard Freeman with the breed she helped establish in the U.S. (Charles Goodman)

The first AKC Champions of Record were recorded in January

Rottweilers have a long history of excelling in performance events like obedience trials. Am/Can CH Von Gailingen's Dassie Did It, UDT, CanCD, follows in their footsteps. (Thompson)

1949. They were littermates CH Zero, owned by Noel Paul Jones of California, and CH Zola, owned by Erna Pinkerton of California. Zero's and Zola's pedigrees can be traced back to the first AKC-registered litter.

Some of the earliest Rottweiler kennels were Mr. A. Knecht's Wellwood, the Hermann's Crestwood, Mrs. Geraldine Dodge's Giralda, Mr. Herman Heid's Von Hohenreissach, the Rademacher-Klem's Rodsden, the DeVore's Follow Me, Mr. Eugene Schoelkopf's Palos Park, Mr. William Stahl's Von Stahl, Ms. Felice Luburich's Srigo, Mrs. Bernard Freeman's Freeger and Mrs. Barbara Hoard's Panamint. Many Rottweiler pedigrees today can be traced back to these American foundation kennels—our Von Gailingen and Lindenwood Rottweilers certainly can. American Rottweiler breeders today should appreciate the dedication to the Rottweiler these early breeders had, especially when you realize that, unlike today, the Rottweiler was not very popular and, in fact, in 1960, only 77 Rottweilers were registered by the AKC.

FROM NOT TO HOT

The Rottweiler started to gain in popularity in the mid '80s. Why did the popularity of the Rottweiler soar? There are many reasons: his looks, his strong character, his easy keeping. Society was also creating a demand for guard dogs. As people moved out of the cities and into the suburbs, they had a place to keep a large dog and, of course, the thieves followed them to suburbia. The Rottweiler was a fairly rare breed and thus became somewhat fashionable for the yuppies of the '80s. Then there was and still is the greed factor. Many people decided to reproduce Rottweilers for cash. As this unique breed became easy to obtain and people had more disposable income, its popularity soared even higher. As his popularity rose, his purchase price came down, and that allowed even more people to purchase the Rottweiler. The Rottweiler's surge in popularity

With a face like this, it's no wonder the Rottweiler is such a popular dog!

started refusing homeowners' insurance. This fact alone has scared people away from the large guard-type breeds.

During the '60s and '70s, because of his almost rare breed status and resulting high purchase price (back then, any Rottweiler brought between $350 and $500, and other purebred dogs were fetching between $50 to $100), many celebrities chose the Rottweiler as their house dogs or guardians. The first celebrity Cathy met with Rottweilers was Doc Severinson of *The Tonight Show.* Cathy was attending the Quarter Horse Congress with her Natascha, and this personable man came up and

did not just occur in the U.S. but internationally as well. This phenomenon has made the Rottweiler one of the most popular breeds in the world.

The Rottweiler was about eightieth in popularity in 1980 and rose to number two by the early '90s. As bites and maulings by Rottweilers rose, their popularity started to wane. Although Rottweilers are still number two, the last two years have seen a drop of about 20 percent in registrations. Going back to the bites and maulings, owners of any breed whose numbers go up also see a corresponding increase in the number of bites. With the increase in bites, insurance companies

Fortunately for responsible Rottweiler breeders and owners, some of the difficulties of owning a large guard-type dog have caused the breed's numbers to decrease slightly. (Marge Gold)

started talking about his dogs, purchased from Felice Luberich's Srigo Kennels. After a short chat, he left. Cathy's friends asked her if she knew who that man was. She replied that she didn't, but he sure had cute little bugles on his boots.

FAMOUS OWNERS

Other famous folks that share their homes with Rottweilers are former West German Chancellor Konrad Adenauer, Walter Mondale, Benson Ford, Geraldine Rockefeller Dodge, Buck Owens, Burt Reynolds, John Madden, Will Smith and Jada Pinkett, Shannon Doherty, Adrian Paul, Canadian Wayne Rostad,

Corey Louckily (left) and Mark Maddox are two Buffalo Bills football players who love Rottweilers. (Grupp)

Good Dog Carl author Alexandra Day, and professional athletes Shaquille O'Neal, Scottie Pippin, Jerry Rice, Herschel Walker, Carlton Bailey, Penny Hardaway, Ken Griffey, Jr. and Deion Sanders.

The Rottweiler of today still possesses the working, guarding and companion abilities so desired in the development of the breed. These characteristics can only be preserved through careful breeding of dogs who are allowed to work and who demonstrate the soundness, temperament and type of the Utility Dogs who became known as the Rottweiler.

(Terry Vavra Photography)

CHAPTER 3

Official Standard of the Rottweiler

The 1990 American Kennel Club Standard is the official document that describes the ideal Rottweiler for fanciers in the United States. It is also the guide for U.S. breeders and judges in selecting breeding stock for future generations of dogs. The *Federation Cynologic Internationale* (FCI), the European organization that regulates dog shows around the world, also has a Rottweiler standard. The FCI standard is written by the *Algemeiner Deutsche Rottweiler Klub* (ADRK). Just as the American Rottweiler Club controls the AKC standard, the ADRK controls the FCI standard. Both documents are quite close, with only small variations; the biggest difference between them is that the AKC standard allows for a single missing tooth, and the FCI standard does not allow any missing teeth.

Because breed standards are official documents that describe the ideal, we have tried to make understanding the standard easier by providing not only the official text, but also an "interpretation" of the text. The official standard is printed in regular type, and the interpretation is below it in italicized type.

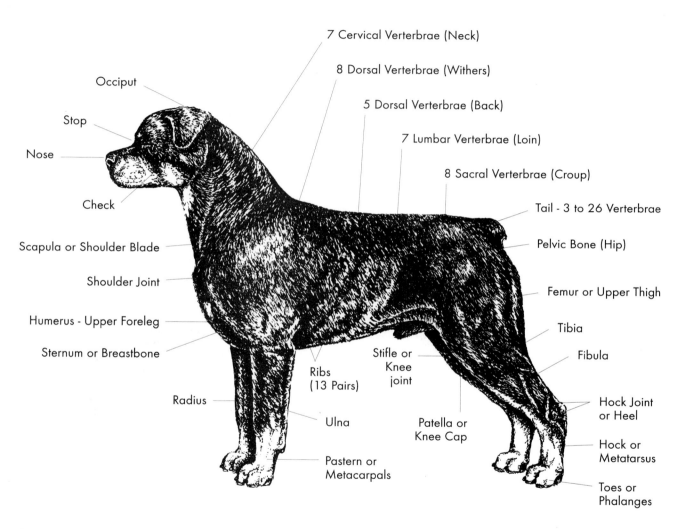

7 Cervical Verterbrae (Neck)

8 Dorsal Verterbrae (Withers)

5 Dorsal Verterbrae (Back)

7 Lumbar Verterbrae (Loin)

8 Sacral Verterbrae (Croup)

Tail - 3 to 26 Verterbrae

Pelvic Bone (Hip)

Femur or Upper Thigh

Tibia

Fibula

Hock Joint or Heel

Hock or Metatarsus

Toes or Phalanges

Occiput

Stop

Nose

Check

Scapula or Shoulder Blade

Shoulder Joint

Humerus - Upper Foreleg

Sternum or Breastbone

Radius

Ribs (13 Pairs)

Ulna

Pastern or Metacarpals

Stifle or Knee joint

Patella or Knee Cap

Reprinted with permission from the ARC.

THE AKC STANDARD OF THE ROTTWEILER

GENERAL APPEARANCE—The ideal Rottweiler is a medium-large, robust and powerful dog; he is black with clearly defined rust markings. His compact and substantial build denotes great strength, agility and endurance. Dogs are characteristically more massive throughout, with a larger frame and heavier bone than bitches. Bitches are distinctly feminine but without weakness of substance or structure.

The preceding paragraph describes the overall picture of the Rottweiler. It clearly says that the Rottweiler is an athletic dog. You should picture a canine athlete, somewhat like a heavyweight fighter or football running back. The Rottweiler is very muscular—not overweight or tall and thin like a marathon racer or football corner.

SIZE, PROPORTION, SUBSTANCE—*Size*—Dogs, 24 inches to 27 inches. Bitches, 22 inches to 25 inches, with the preferred size being mid-range of each sex.

Proportion—Correct proportion is of primary importance, as long as size is within the standard's range. The length of body, from prosternum to the rearmost projection of the rump, is slightly longer than the height of the dog at the withers, the most desirable proportion of the height to length being 9 to 10. *Substance*—The Rottweiler is neither coarse nor shelly. Depth of chest is approximately 50 percent of the height of the dog. His bone and muscle mass must be sufficient to balance his frame, giving a compact and very powerful appearance. *Serious faults*—Lack of proportion, undersized, oversized, reversal of sex characteristics (bitchy dogs, doggy bitches).

Am/Can CH Rodsden's Lindenwood Hero, CD, VB, TT, gives the compact and powerful appearance called for in the standard. (Ashbey)

The adult Rottweiler is the canine athletic equivalent of a heavyweight fighter or football player.

The preceding paragraph is probably the most important one of the standard. It describes the height. It describes the ratio of height to length. It describes the Rottweiler as being substantial, with great muscle and bone strength. It describes his body as deep.

A correct Rottweiler must have correct-to-the-standard body proportions. It is the body proportions that give a clear picture of the breed and separate it from other breeds. The Rottweiler standard describes a nearly square dog. If this nearly square dog is also to be an athletic dog, then balance between the body parts is essential.

Later paragraphs of the standard describe the fore and rear quarters; if you remember that the ideal Rottweiler is nearly square, what is described will become even more important.

The FCI standard says that the length of the Rottweiler should not exceed the height by, at most, 15 percent. This statement allows a dog to be an inch longer than the AKC standard allows.

This bitch has the desired self-assured expression, almond-shaped eyes and broadness between the ears called for in the standard.

HEAD—Of medium length, broad between the ears; forehead line seen in profile is moderately arched; zygomatic arch and stop well-developed, with strong, broad upper and lower jaws. The desired ratio of backskull to muzzle is 3 to 2. Forehead is preferred dry; however, some wrinkling may occur when the dog is alert. *Expression*—Noble, alert, and self-assured. *Eyes*—Medium size, almond shaped, with well-fitting lids, moderately deep set, neither protruding nor receding. The desired color is a uniform dark brown. *Serious faults*—Yellow (bird of prey) eyes, eyes of different color or size, hairless eye rim. *Disqualification*—Entropion, ectropion.

EARS—Medium size, pendant, triangular; when carried alertly, the ears are level with the top of the skull and appear to broaden it. Ears are to be set well apart, hanging forward, with the inner edge lying tightly against the head and terminating at approximately mid-cheek. *Serious faults*—Improper carriage (creased, folded or held away from cheek/head). *Muzzle*—Bridge is straight, broad at base with light tapering toward tip. End of the muzzle is broad with well-developed chin. Nose is broad rather than round and always black. *Lips*—Always black; corners closed; inner mouth pigment is preferred dark. *Serious faults*—Total lack of mouth pigment (pink mouth). *Bite and dentition*—Teeth 42 in number (20 upper, 22 lower), strong, correctly placed, meeting in a scissors bite—lower incisors touching inside of upper incisors. *Serious faults*—Level bite; any missing tooth. *Disqualification*—Overshot, undershot (when incisors do not touch or mesh); wry mouth; two or more missing teeth.

Her head is nice, but this bitch has the serious faults of creased ears and lack of mouth pigment.

Excellent mouth pigmentation and strong teeth. Note that all four premolars and first molar on lower jaw can be easily seen when the dog is panting.

The two standards are nearly identical when it comes to describing the head, muzzle, lips and mouth pigment. The correct Rottweiler head is very strong and dry—in other words, without any extra skin. The muzzle starts at the corners of the eyes and only slightly tapers to the nose. The end of the muzzle is wide and somewhat blunt. The bluntness is the result of a combination of placement of the teeth, some padding of the lips and a strong lower jaw, showing a chin.

As mentioned before, the major difference in the two standards is that the AKC allows for a single missing tooth, and the FCI standard disqualifies for it. Other differences are that the FCI standard also disqualifies for eyes that are of different color or too yellow, whereas the AKC standard lists these as serious faults. The FCI standard lists ears that are low set, heavy, long, slack, flying or not carried symmetrically as faults.

NECK, TOPLINE, SUBSTANCE—*Neck*—Powerful, well-muscled, moderately long, slightly arched without loose skin. *Topline*—The back is firm and level, extending in a straight line from behind the withers to the croup. The back remains horizontal to the ground while the dog is moving or standing. *Body*—The chest is roomy, broad and deep, reaching to elbow, with well-pronounced forechest and well-sprung, oval ribs. Back is straight and strong. Loin is short, deep and well-muscled. Croup is broad, of medium length and only slightly sloping. Underline of a mature Rottweiler has a slight tuckup. Males must have two normal testicles properly descended into the scrotum. *Disqualification*—Unilateral cryptorchid or cryptorchid males. *Tail*—Tail docked short, close to body, leaving one or two vertebrae. The set of the tail is more important than length. Properly set, it gives an impression of elongation of topline; carried slightly above horizontal when the dog is excited or moving.

This year-old dog has a lovely head and expression, but his ears are large.

A class of Rottweiler bitches being shown in Scandinavia—note the natural tails! (Piusz)

This section of the two standards is virtually identical. Because some European countries have banned tail docking (on May 1, 1998, most of Europe banned docking) the FCI standard has a clause on the Rottweiler's natural tail that states "the tail may be in its natural state." This does not really describe what the German club thinks is a correctly set tail or a tail that is carried naturally. There are pictures of Scandinavian Rottweilers with tails, and the carriage is all over the place, curled over the back, hanging down like a Labrador Retriever, and so on. Because Rottweilers were never selected for tail carriage or type, this is to be expected when tail docking is suddenly ceased. During one of the International Friends of the Rottweiler meetings in 1993, the ADRK said the Rottweiler tail should be like that of the Greater Swiss Mountain Dog. Because of the recent changes in Germany banning the docking of tails, the ADRK must further clarify the set and carriage of the natural tail.

FOREQUARTERS—Shoulder blade is long and well-laid back. Upper arm equal in length to shoulder blade, set so elbows are well under body. Distance from withers to elbow and elbow to ground is equal. Legs are strongly developed with straight, heavy bone, not set close together. Pasterns are strong, springy and almost perpendicular to the ground. Feet are round, compact with well-arched toes, turning neither in nor out. Pads are thick and hard. Nails are short, strong and black. Dewclaws may be removed.

The American standard describes the front assembly in more detail than the FCI standard. It tells of correct leg length, length and angle of the upper arm and length of the shoulder blade. There are no discrepancies between the standards on the forequarters. Both standards describe the required conformation of an athletic dog.

Australian Champion Callirhowe Rudi Voeler shows off his forequarters.

The reason the standard goes into such detail on the front assembly is because the Rottweiler is nearly square, and if he is to move correctly, he must have a correct front. This is a front that allows for a long, effortless stride. The angles and length of bones mentioned, as well as the long, well-angulated shoulder matched with a long, well-angled upper arm, are so the Rottweiler will possess the required length of stride called for in a trotting dog of great endurance and agility.

HINDQUARTERS—Angulation of hindquarters balances that of forequarters. Upper thigh is fairly long, very broad and well-muscled. Stifle joint is well-turned. Lower thigh is long, broad and powerful, with extensive muscling leading into a strong hock joint. Rear pasterns are nearly perpendicular to the ground. Viewed from the rear, hind legs are straight, strong and wide enough apart to fit with a properly built body. Back feet are somewhat longer than front feet, turning neither in nor out, equally compact with well-arched toes. Pads are thick and hard. Nails short, strong and black. Dewclaws must be removed.

The first sentence in this section says it all. Balance, balance, balance! The two halves of the dog must be in balance with each other for correct movement. With the nearly square profile called for in the standard, it is even more important that the dog is balanced. An underdone rear with a correct front limits the dog to pulling himself forward—a very tiring task. An overdone rear assembly overpowers the front, requiring the dog to move sideways or to do other things to keep his legs from interfering. All these adjustments to compensate for lack of balance reduce endurance and agility.

The difference between the AKC and FCI standards on the hindquarters has to do with dewclaws. The FCI standard says that it is considered a fault if rear dewclaws are present. The AKC standard says that rear dewclaws must be removed. Some breeders think that the presence of a functional extra rear toe (a dewclaw that has a formed joint versus a dewclaw attached by skin only) causes the rear pastern to twist. This gives the dog the appearance of being cowhocked. This is thought to be true even if the dewclaw is removed.

COAT—Outer coat is straight, coarse, dense, of medium length and lying flat. Undercoat should be present on neck and thighs, but the amount is influenced by climatic conditions. However, Rottweilers who live in the southern United States will have less undercoat present than Rottweilers from colder climates. Undercoat should not show through outer coat. The coat is shortest on the head, ears and legs,

To be the versatile athlete he is, the Rottweiler's front and hindquarters must balance so he can move more correctly. This is CH Seren's Renaissance Man running an agility course with his owner J. Parker. (J.K. Lentini)

some waves over the croup. Usually this is transient, depending on the amount of undercoat. A faulty coat may also be one that has cowlicks. These cowlicks often make the coat, especially on the shoulders and upper arm, grow in the wrong direction and give a rough appearance to the coat.

The more serious faults deal with coats that limit the dog's ability to work in adverse weather. The open coat allows moisture to sink down to the skin. A wet dog is usually a cold dog and one not willing or able to work.

The same is true for the excessively short coat. With little or no undercoat, there is no insulation for extreme heat or cold, again limiting the dog's ability to perform. The curly coat referred to in the American standard is the one the FCI standard disqualifies. This is a Rottweiler whose coat has deep waves from head to toe, rather like a marcel potato chip. The waves may be so deep that they tend to curl.

Neither standard mentions a wire coat, like that of the Schnauzers. This type of coat does appear infrequently. Any Rottweiler with such a coat should not be shown and should definitely not be bred.

COLOR—Always black with rust-to-mahogany markings. The demarcation between black and

and is longest on the breeching. The Rottweiler is to be exhibited in the natural condition, with no trimming. *Fault*—Wavy coat. *Serious faults*—Open, excessively short or curly coat; total lack of undercoat; any trimming that alters the length of the natural coat. *Disqualification*—Long coat.

You must remember that the Rottweiler was bred to work in a cold, damp climate. The standard calls for a double coat—a coarse, flat outer coat covering a short, thick undercoat. Any condition of the coat that limits the dog's ability to work in adverse weather conditions is very faulty. There is much discussion and debate over the term wavy. The AKC standard lists a wavy coat as a simple fault; the FCI standard calls for a wavy coat to be disqualified, and it also lists it as a fault. Obviously this is a matter of semantics. The American definition of a wavy coat is one that has

These seven-month-old littermates have the correct coat as described in the standard. (Thompson)

A long coat is a disqualifying fault; some puppies in the same litter will have it while the others won't, like the pup on the far right.

rust is to be clearly defined. The markings should be located as follows: a spot over each eye; on the cheeks; as a strip around each side of the muzzle, but not on the bridge of the nose; on the throat; a triangular mark on both sides of the prosternum; on the forelegs from the carpus downward to the toes; on the inside of the rear legs showing down the front of the stifle and broadening out to the front of the rear legs from the hock to toes, but not completely eliminating black from the rear of pasterns; under the tail; penciling on toes. The undercoat is gray, tan or black. Quantity and location of rust markings is important and should not exceed 10 percent of the body color. *Serious faults*—Straw-colored, excessive, insufficient or sooty markings; rust marking other than described above; white marking any place on dog (a few rust or white hairs do not constitute a marking). *Disqualification*—Any base color other than black; absence of all markings.

This section of the standard is really pretty straightforward. The AKC lists white markings as a serious fault, and the

Having a correct coat is important because it enables the Rottweiler to work outdoors in all types of weather. (Peter Florence)

FCI standard calls for disqualification. Because of the Rottweiler's close heritage to the Swiss tri-colored breeds, it is not unusual for puppies to be born with white markings. These markings usually are located on the chest or under the chin. Occasionally, pups are born with white toes. Again, these dogs should not be shown or bred. Granted, these markings are cosmetic in nature, but the Rottweiler is a black and tan dog, period.

GAIT—The Rottweiler is a trotter. His movement should be balanced, harmonious, sure, powerful and unhindered, with a strong forereach and powerful

Note how the markings vary on these dogs, yet all are correct. (Welkerhaus)

aloofness that does not lend itself to immediate and indiscriminate friendships. A Rottweiler is self-confident and responds quietly and with a wait-and-see attitude to influences in his environment. He has an inherent desire to protect home and family, and he is an intelligent dog of extreme hardness and adaptability with a strong willingness to work, making him especially suited as a companion, guardian and general all-purpose dog.

The behavior of the Rottweiler in the show ring should be controlled, willing and adaptable, and trained to submit to examination of the mouth, testicles, and so on. An aloof or reserved dog should not be penalized because this reflects the accepted character of the breed. An aggressive or belligerent attitude toward other dogs should not be faulted.

rear drive. The motion is effortless, efficient and ground-covering. Front and rear legs are thrown neither in nor out because the imprint of the hind feet should touch that of the forefeet. In a trot, the forequarters and hindquarters are mutually coordinated while the back remains level, firm and relatively motionless. As speed increases, the legs converge under the body toward a center line.

Once again, the standard describes a correctly moving, athletic dog. If the Rottweiler is to be true to his heritage of a multipurpose dog, he must move with power and ease. Because of his heavy bone and musculature, he must move effortlessly and in a most efficient way, or he will tire and fail to perform. The FCI standard does not address correct movement. However, in European shows, the dogs are side-gaited for a very long time, so proper movement is certainly assessed and given a high priority.

TEMPERAMENT—The Rottweiler is basically a calm, confident and courageous dog with a self-assured

A newborn puppy showing large white markings on the chest, similar to the white markings on the Swiss breeds with which the Rottweiler shares his heritage.

CORRECT AND INCORRECT GAITS
AS DEPICTED IN THE ARC ILLUSTRATED STANDARD.

Breaking Behind Withers

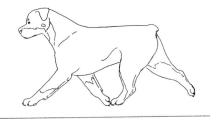

Pacing

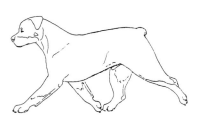

Moving Downhill

Lack of Reach and Drive

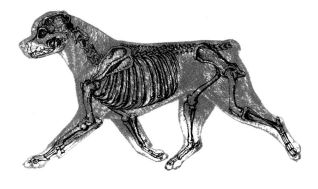

Correct gait

Reprinted with permission from the ARC.

A judge will excuse from the ring any shy Rottweiler. A dog will be judged fundamentally shy if, refusing to stand for examination, it shrinks away from the judge. A dog that, in the opinion of the judge, menaces or threatens him or her, or exhibits any sign that it may not be safely approached or examined by the judge in the normal manner will be excused from the ring. A dog that, in the opinion of the judge, attacks any person in the ring will be disqualified.

The two standards are in complete agreement on the correct temperament of the Rottweiler. The FCI standard is most demanding in good temperament and character. It disqualifies any Rottweiler that is anxious, shy, cowardly, gun-shy, vicious, excessively suspicious or nervous.

You can tell this mother-daughter—CH Freeger's Juno, CD, and Freeger's Priska—have the kind of temperaments described in the standard. (Freeman)

In trying to get a picture of what a Rottweiler should look like and act like, it helps to have dogs like Am/Can CH Bluewater's Zeus Von Zolty, CD, JHD, DsH I to look at. (Glynn and Goodwin)

These three dogs are showing well and appear to have correct temperaments. The judge will decide.

The AKC standard, in summary, states the following:

FAULTS—The foregoing is a description of the ideal Rottweiler. Any structural fault that detracts from the above described working dog must be penalized to the extent of the deviation.

All this paragraph says is that structural faults must be penalized. The FCI standard has a long list of structural faults. This summary sentence eliminates the need for such a list.

The final section of the AKC standard is the list of disqualifications. This is also true of the FCI standard.

Here are both lists:

DISQUALIFICATIONS

AKC	FCI
Entropion, ectropion; marked reversal of sex type—for example, feminine dogs or masculine bitches.	Entropion, ectropion; yellow eyes, different colored eyes.
Overshot, undershot (when incisors do not touch or mesh); wry mouth; two or more missing teeth.	Overshot or undershot bite; wry mouth; missing one incisor, one canine, one premolar or one molar.
Unilateral cryptorchid or apparently normal testicles fully descended into the scrotum.	Males must have two cryptorchid testicles
Long coat.	Coat texture: very long or wavy.
Any base color other than black; absence of all black; absence of all markings.	Coat color: Dogs that do not show the typical Rottweiler coloring of black with tan markings. White markings.
A dog that, in the opinion of the judge, attacks any person in the ring.	Behavior: Anxious, shy, cowardly, gun-shy, vicious, excessively suspicious, nervous animals.

To fully understand the picture of the ideal dog that breed standards attempt to describe, it is necessary to attend breed seminars and find mentors who can show you as many examples of a "good Rottweiler" as possible. Mental pictures are often not intuitively obvious from word descriptions, so there is no substitute for observing Rottweilers not only in the show ring, but at work as well.

(Close Encounters of the Furry Kind/T. Harrison)

CHAPTER 4

Finding the Right Dog— Puppy, Adult or Rescue

Rottweiler Puppies: massive bone, parents on premises, family-raised, x-rayed, champion bloodlines. Call 555-666-7777.

If you're looking for a Rottweiler, should you call this number? This ad is typical of ads found in local papers across the country. In our opinion, there is no harm in calling; all the information you can gather in your search is good. It is what you do with that information that is important.

Now back to that ad. What does it mean? Do the puppies have massive bone? You do not know unless the breeder is very experienced and knows what this combination of parents produces. What does "parents on premises" mean? Are both the sire and dam of the puppies owned by the breeder? Do both live in the house? Are both approachable? *Approachable* means you get to meet and greet both the sire and the dam. Why were these two animals bred with each other? Was it a matter of convenience? Were these puppies produced to show the children the miracle of life or to make a little money? Was there any planning in producing this litter? Or does "parents on premises" simply mean that the father and mother of the human family live there?

When you're shopping for a puppy, find out as much about the pup's parents as you can. (Thompson)

What does "family-raised" mean? Does this mean that breeders with kennels do not raise well-socialized pups? Does this mean that the pups are in the basement and the family lives above them with no interaction? Are the family's children allowed to play and interact with the pups?

What does "x-rayed" mean? Does it mean that the mother once broke a leg and had an x-ray taken? Does it mean that the puppies have been x-rayed for some reason? Ask to see certificates from the *Orthopedic Foundation for Animals* (OFA) if that is what the ad is referring to.

What does "champion bloodlines" mean? Does it mean that the puppies' great-great grandfather had a championship? There is no mention of the parents being champions or having working titles.

More important, there is no mention of health checks.

THINK HEALTH FIRST

When you call the phone number in an ad such as this, you really need to ask all the questions mentioned here. Especially, you need to ask about health checks. You should ask to see the certificates for hips and elbows, eyes and heart. Do not just take a breeder's word that these checks were done. The owner of the sire of the litter should have given copies of the appropriate certificates to the owner of the dam. These health checks are routinely done by quality breeders. When you purchase a pup, you want it to be healthy, not just at seven or eight weeks, but for its lifetime. Having all the proper health checks on the parents will not guarantee that your pup will grow up without problems, but it sure hedges your bet.

Make sure your puppy is healthy all over—appearance and genes!

Puppies should be raised with lots of human interaction. Where they are physically whelped or raised does not matter as much as how they are raised. There must be lots of human attention lavished on them.

The experience of the breeder also matters. Someone with his first litter is not as knowledgeable as a breeder of long standing. Experience in picking breeding partners, raising the litter, and knowing how pups grow and develop enables experienced breeders to answer many of the puppy buyer's questions.

EXPECT QUESTIONS

Be very wary if a Rottweiler breeder does not ask you a lot of questions. Responsible breeders take care to place puppies and adults in good homes. They want to understand what the potential owner really wants to do with a Rottweiler. Expect questions like these:

- Have you ever owned a Rottweiler before? What happened to him?

- If you've never owned a Rottweiler, have you owned a dog? If so, what breed? How long did you have him?

- Do you have any pets currently? If so, what kind? Who takes care of them?

- Do you have children at home? What are their ages? Have they ever been around animals?

- Are you expecting to have a baby in the near future?

- Will there ever be a time when the children will be alone to care for a Rottweiler—for example, after school?

- Does anyone in your household have allergies to dogs?

- Do you live in an apartment or a house? Do you own or rent? If you rent, are large dogs allowed, especially Rottweilers?

- Do you have a fenced yard?

- Can you exercise a Rottweiler daily? How?

- Do you know the dog laws in your community?

- Are you prepared for the expense of purchasing quality dog food, veterinary care, boarding when you're away and obedience classes?

- Describe a perfect day with a Rottweiler.

Healthy puppies raised right will have had lots of human contact.

Expect to be asked a lot of question by a responsible breeder before he or she decides a pup is right for you.

A responsible Rottweiler breeder will aptitude-test a litter. He will observe the litter and try to match a puppy's basic disposition with the buyer's needs. For example, if you want a Rottweiler who can compete in obedience competitions, the breeder will steer you toward a puppy who has a keen interest in working with people and is not extremely dominant. If you have young children, a Rottweiler puppy with a high pain tolerance and lower prey drive will be a good choice. If you are elderly or arthritic, a Rottweiler with a low pain tolerance will be a good choice. If you're a novice puppy buyer and the breeder lets you pick a puppy with no guidance, buy a puppy elsewhere. If you think of all the great dogs you've known, it is not the coat and color that make them great, it's their personality and natural tendencies and how they suit your lifestyle.

When you see a litter of Rottweiler puppies, you should expect to see miniature versions of adult Rottweilers. Their ear carriage, head and body proportions and bites will be the same at seven weeks as seven years. Older puppies will change proportions and go through "Dachshund" stages. They also may develop "flying" ears, pointed heads and strange fronts at five months in some bloodlines. If you are looking at puppies who are four months to one year, and you are looking for a show prospect, you must observe the sire and dam and trust that the breeder knows the development of his bloodlines. Rottweiler puppies gain as much as 100 pounds in their first year, which does cause rather strange growth spurts.

THE SALES CONTRACT

When you purchase a Rottweiler, you should receive a sales contract that fully explains what you are buying and from whom. This contract may also

Rottweiler puppies are miniature versions of adults—these guys will soon be much bigger!

contain things the buyer has to do and things the breeder will do for the buyer. Is it mandatory to neuter your pup, take it to obedience classes or enter dog shows? Is the puppy being sold on a limited registration? Does the breeder demand that the dog be returned if it needs to be re-homed? Will the breeder take the pup back in a few days and offer a full refund if things do not work out?

Sometimes the sales contract also includes guarantees. You need to be sure that you understand these guarantees. Chapter 6 explains what the health terms mean. No breeder gives two pups for the price of one. So a guarantee for an OFA hip clearance does not mean that you get a free puppy if your dog has hip dysplasia. Find out right away what the guarantee means to you if your dog's hips do not clear OFA with a number. Most breeders will sell you another dog at a reduced price or refund a part of the purchase price. Some Rottweiler breeders will give you another dog, but only if you return the first one. Most puppy owners are not willing to return their first dog after living with it for over two years. There may also be a demand that you neuter your dog before anything is done. All these things need to be addressed when you purchase your puppy.

If you are purchasing a show prospect, are there guarantees for disqualifying faults? If so, what are they? Sometimes with show prospects, there is a co-ownership option. You need to fully understand what is involved with co-ownership. Who is the co-owner? What is the co-owner responsible for? Why is there a co-ownership? Are you paying top dollar and giving future pups to the co-owner? This often makes the sale price rather high.

No matter which puppy ends up going home with you, he should include a sales contract from the breeder.

THE PEDIGREE

When you get your puppy, reputable breeders have a pedigree for the pup. They should go over it with you to familiarize you with the titles and dogs it contains. (You must do your homework before this is discussed, however, so you can know that the breeder actually understands the titles himself. Linda once had a breeder tell her that CD meant Champion Dog.) The breeder should teach you how to read a pedigree if you do not already know how to read one. The breeder may also provide you with photos of the puppy's parents and even grandparents.

Most breeders will give you a diet sheet and list of shots and wormings your new pup has received. They will go over each list with you so that you understand them. They will also answer any questions you have and make recommendations for

Make sure the breeder goes over your pup's pedigree with you, especially if she's a show prospect.

registering your puppy. Many Rottweiler owners will name all of the puppies and register each one individually prior to placing any of the pups. This ensures that their naming scheme is intact. Don't be offended by this common practice; appreciate that the breeder is proud to have his kennel name associated with this puppy.

At what age should you get a Rottweiler puppy, or should you consider an older dog? No puppy should be released from the rest of the litter until seven weeks of age. How much older does not matter too much if the pup is being raised where it is getting lots of human contact.

Many times, breeders will keep a puppy only to find that it does not grow to meet the desired potential. Perhaps it develops a bad bite or other disqualification and the breeder now wants to

Because puppies learn important lessons from their dam and littermates, it's wise not to separate them before the pup is at least seven weeks old.

quality dog-food brands, amounts to feed and shots that your puppy needs.

REGISTRATION PAPERS

You should receive registration papers when you take your puppy home. Be wary if papers are promised later. You will also find that it is customary for Rottweiler breeders to require that their kennel name and, often, a name beginning with a designated letter of the alphabet be used when

You may want to purchase an older dog, like this six-month-old who may not make it as a show dog, but can be a great pet.

place the youngster. If this pup has been well-socialized, there is usually no problem with it adjusting to a new home. Many times, getting an older dog is a blessing. The dog is leashbroken, housebroken and beyond the chewing stage. For some households this is a real plus, especially if there is no one home during the day or you live in an apartment.

Be aware of *kennel dog syndrome*. This refers to dogs who have had little or no human contact. They are very fearful of new surroundings and have no idea how to relate to humans. With a tremendous amount of patience and working with the dog, it may come out of its shell. If the dog was isolated, not only from humans, but other dogs as well, it may not even know how to deal with

other canines. These dogs do not do well as pets and should be avoided at all costs. Kennel dog syndrome does not apply to all older dogs—it just applies to dogs that have not been properly raised and socialized.

ROTTWEILER RESCUE

Potential buyers of older dogs may want to consider a rescue. There are many great Rottweilers out there looking for a new family. Some, through no fault of their own, must find new owners. Some, through cruelty or neglect, are in desperate need of loving families.

The negative side of rescue is that in many cases not much individual history of the dog is available. The pedigree is not known, therefore the health background of the ancestors is blank. You do not know the temperament of the ancestors or the way in which the dog was raised or trained. If you are interested in rescuing a Rottweiler, contact your local Rottweiler club, the American Rottweiler Club or the American Kennel Club's breeder referral line. There are many rescue groups, and a breeder or club member should be able to refer you to one.

BOY OR GIRL?

What sex Rottweiler should you purchase? You should get the sex you prefer. There are many loving, gentle males as well as females who are great with children and other pets. If the male is what attracted you to the breed or if you simply prefer males, then get a male. The Rottweiler male is

The start your Rottweiler gets in life will make a big difference in what kind of dog he grows up to be—that's why it's wise to buy from a reputable breeder.

Male or female, it's up to you—each Rottweiler is an individual.

bigger and more imposing. He sometimes can be more talkative (growly) and independent than Rottweiler bitches. If the breed is right for you, then the sex should not matter. You should be able to find the right Rottweiler of either sex for you and your family. If you are intimidated by the male Rottweiler, then you really should think about another breed.

Many books and magazines advise the potential owner to buy from a breeder. So where do you find a reputable Rottweiler breeder? You can contact the American Kennel Club, which will put you in touch with the American Rottweiler Club's breeder referral service. (See Appendix A, "Organizations and Other Resources," for addresses and phone numbers.) You can contact some breeders on the Internet—but be careful. You can meet with breeders at dog shows. When you go to a dog show, please remember that the breeders there are really nervous or are busy showing their dogs, so just ask for a card so that you can call them at a more convenient time. Some states have Federations of Dog

Clubs or individual kennel clubs that publish breeders' directories. These directories are available at local veterinarians' offices and libraries. Other experts recommend rescuing Rottweilers.

Back to the ad at the beginning of this chapter: Remember, responsible breeders usually do not have to advertise in the classifieds. Their breedings are carefully planned, and they tend to have puppy buyers lined up even before the mating.

One last statement on finding the right Rottweiler for you: Acquiring a Rottweiler is a family decision. If all family members do not want a Rottweiler, do not get one.

Your Rottweiler is going to be a member of the family, so make sure everyone wants him before you get him.

(Roger LeMar)

CHAPTER 5

Living with a Rottweiler

Living with a Rottweiler is a truly rewarding experience, providing fun, humor and companionship— if you are a responsible dog owner and are willing to invest the time and energy to properly train and socialize your dog. The Rottweiler is not for everyone, especially if you are unwilling or unable to share your house, family and life with a large dog. Living with an unsocialized, untrained, bored, unhappy Rottweiler will not be enjoyable for you, your family or your neighbors.

What is it like to live with a well-socialized, trained Rottweiler? You will laugh. You will cry. You will feel more secure. You will never walk from room to room alone again. You will vacuum and sweep up dog hair. You will buy a wardrobe that doesn't show black dog hair. You will begin to decorate your house with colors and patterns that do not show black dog hair or big, muddy footprints. You will become more physically affectionate. You will become more assertive. You will get your feet stepped on. You will learn to extol the virtues of a Rottweiler to your friends and neighbors who are afraid to come near your house. You will become an expert on homeowner's insurance and where to get it. You will have the time of your life.

What do you need to know about living with a Rottweiler? First, whether your Rottweiler is a puppy or an adult, he should live in your house. Rottweilers need companionship and enjoy sharing your daily activities. A Rottweiler who is left outside all day will create his own pastimes, including digging, chewing and chasing the neighbors along the fence (you must have a fence; never keep him on a chain; never let him run free). The unattended Rottweiler in your yard is also a target for theft.

Life with a Rottweiler can be a ball, as this 12-year-old dog proves. (Michels)

While on the topic of theft, let us broach the subject of individually identifying your Rottweiler so that if he is lost or stolen he can be returned to you. There are basically two ways of permanent identification. The first is tattooing. The problem with tattoos is that if placed in an ear, the ear can be removed! If placed on the belly, no one is brave enough to roll a strange adult Rottweiler over to read it!

The second method is to use a microchip. A microchip is a teeny-weeny computer chip that is implanted under the dog's skin at the base of the neck. This chip is readable by a scanner. Strange adult Rottweilers can be scanned easily. Most local veterinarians carry and implant microchips. Whether your dog is tattooed or microchipped makes no difference. What is important is that the microchip number or tattoo is registered with a national registry. As of this writing, the AKC's

Home Again microchip program of returning lost dogs has been 100 percent effective. Beyond using one of these permanent methods, you should also have a simple ID tag for your dog's collar. It's the first thing people look for when they come across a lost dog.

A CLOSE COMPANION

A Rottweiler in your house will be entertaining. Rottweilers want to be with you every minute. If you or your children like to lay on the floor to watch TV, your Rottweiler will lay beside you. If you are sick and in bed, your Rottweiler will lay beside your bed. Rottweilers enjoy helping you load the dishwasher, fold the laundry and most of all, accompany you to the bathroom. A well-known breeder has admitted that she teaches her dogs to show their bite while she's sitting on the toilet. Cathy has been known to use this time to teach go-outs. Linda has used this time to inspect ears or check feet.

Rottweilers like to share in all family activities. (Lee Whittier)

Rottweilers like nothing more than to be right beside their special people. (Chuck Tatham/The Standard Image)

Rottweiler, and you will be amazed at how much you can accomplish with these quick sessions.

It is a good idea to keep a supply of treats on hand for such occasions. Some puppies get carried away over treats. If you simply leave your hand in his mouth, yell "ouch," and tell him "easy" or "nice"; he will soon get the idea that he does not have to snatch the treat. Small, easy-to-swallow-without-chewing treats are best. We use an economical treat we refer to as "nuked hot dogs." To prepare them, simply purchase the cheapest hot dogs you can find. Freeze them so that they will be easier to slice. Slice the frozen hot dogs into dime-sized pieces. Place them on a paper towel in the microwave. Cover with another paper towel and nuke them

If you or your guests want privacy in the bathroom, shut the door securely. Rottweilers have a knack for timing; they wait until you are no longer in a position to get up to close the door, then burst open the bathroom door with a "Hey, whatcha doin'" look on their face. This is most distressing for guests, but it will make you laugh.

Having your Rottweiler in the house allows you to hold impromptu training sessions throughout the day. Like most Rottweiler trainers, we do a lot of "kitchen" training. Your Rottweiler can sit before he's given his food dish. Since your Rottweiler will probably accompany you every time you go to the kitchen, you can ask him to sit, down, stand, speak, and so on, then give him a quick reward. This is fun for both you and your

These three happy dogs can't keep their eyes off their owner.

Puppies (and adults) learn quickly when properly motivated, so keep treats on hand for mini training sessions.

for several minutes. The object is to dry them, not fry them into oblivion. The dried slices can be kept in an airtight container in the refrigerator for several weeks.

What will inspire this Rottweiler to "come" from his favorite spot?

Living room training is also handy. Rottweilers love popcorn, and tossing a popped kernel is an easy way to teach your dog to catch or speak. You can work on sit- or down-stays while you and the family are watching TV.

HELPFUL HANDLING

Daily handling is important for Rottweilers. Grooming, nail trimming, bathing, teeth cleaning, showing and trips to the veterinarian all require handling of your Rottweiler by you or someone else. You should touch your puppy or adult

Make sure to give your Rottweiler lots of T.L.C. by handling him gently all over everyday.

Rottweiler all over, every day. Pay particular attention to handling your Rottweiler's feet and toes; besides making it easier to clip nails, you will make it easier for your veterinarian to draw blood and perform other examinations.

If your dog struggles when touched or held, get down to a lower level, like sitting on the floor with him, then reinforce good behavior with praise or a treat when you are done. Increase the time before he gets the treat or praise. Learning to be handled is extremely important; realize that your Rottweiler does not have to enjoy the experience, but he must learn to tolerate it.

Living with a Rottweiler requires proper socialization of your dog. It will help your puppy grow up to be a well-adjusted, confident adult. It should be done while he is still a youngster, especially during the critical period between seven and sixteen weeks old. Socialization means exposing your Rottweiler to a variety of people, places and other dogs. This exposure must be done in an environment that you are in control of—for example, at a puppy training class or while greeting a person while you have your dog on lead. Training classes are an excellent way to socialize, and the class instructor can suggest ways of introducing your Rottweiler to new situations.

Steven and Alex Piusz know how well Rottweilers and children get along—here they pose with seven of their friends. (Piusz)

ROTTWEILERS AND CHILDREN

Probably the most frequent question asked of a Rottweiler owner is "Are they good with children?"

The answer is yes, with proper supervision, socialization and training. First and foremost, never leave your Rottweiler (or any dog, for that matter) alone with children; it does not matter whether the dog is a puppy or an adult. Alexandra Day has written marvelous *Good Dog Carl* books about a Rottweiler who has great adventures with a baby, but please remember that this is a fantasy. No matter how trustworthy your dog is, if unsupervised, he may interpret a situation as dangerous to your child, and his protective instincts may be inappropriate. Likewise, your Rottweiler may need to be protected from the unsupervised child.

Teach your children responsibility by guiding them in how to do things with your Rottweiler. Let your child assist with "kitchen training," which will not only teach your child about handling dogs, but will teach your Rottweiler that he can accept commands by the child. Do teach your child that, when you are present, he or she can ask your dog to sit, then give the dog his food dish, but that the child must never try to take the food dish away or stick his or her hands in the dish when your dog is eating.

Rottweilers weigh more than many adults and all children. Keep this in mind before allowing your child to walk your dog on leash in public places. If you have a toddler, your Rottweiler will probably knock him down. Linda's nieces were both raised with Rottweilers. Both girls, as toddlers, were knocked down by their Rottweilers. Both girls quickly learned to grab the dog as soon as they hit the floor, and the dog would pull them back to their feet. Your neighbor's children and elderly adults can also be knocked down by a well-meaning Rottweiler, so it is important to train your dog that jumping on people is never allowed.

Adult Rottweilers are big dogs; your child may not be strong enough to walk yours in public.

What can you do if you have a Rottweiler and are expecting your first child? First, do not even consider making the house off-limits to your Rottweiler because of the baby. This is not necessary, nor is it fair to the dog. You can condition your Rottweiler to the new arrival before the baby's birth by buying an infant-sized doll and teaching the Rottweiler to be "easy" around the "baby." Allow him to sniff the doll. If he gets too pushy or active, tell him "Easy, the baby." When he settles down, praise him. Do this many times until the dog learns what behavior is appropriate when he is near the "baby." Carry the doll around with you, sit with the doll in your lap and so forth so the dog learns how to behave and the "baby" is not such a big deal. If possible, you can bring one of the real baby's diapers or clothes home (before the baby comes home) to place on the doll. The dog will probably notice the new smell, but since the situation is familiar, you can reinforce the proper behavior easily. When the real baby does come home, your Rottweiler will know what is appropriate, and the adjustment for all of you will be easier. Please remember, do not leave the baby unattended with your dog and remember that your Rottweiler still needs attention, too.

YOUR BIG DOG

The second most frequently asked question is "How much does he weigh?" First of all, bigger Rottweilers are not better Rottweilers. Second of all, most people guess their dog's weight and have no real idea how much he actually weighs. And third, breeders do not raise Rottweilers by the pound and are greatly annoyed by this question. If the weight of the dog is so important to you, it's best to purchase one of the giant breeds; after all, they weigh more than Rottweilers. For those of you who are interested in true Rottweiler weights, a mature male will weigh between 90 and 135 pounds, a mature female between 75 and 100 pounds.

Rottweilers love to play and will even amuse themselves with a big ball they can tackle and chase. (Jim Owens)

A healthy adult male weighs between 90 and 135 pounds— he's a big boy.

TOYS AND GAMES

Rottweilers love toys and games. They will toss toys around and dearly love a good game of tug-of-war. Some "experts" say that you should never play tug-of-war with a dog because it will cause them to become aggressive. Frankly, if you are this

Some find that living with a Rottweiler is so nice they soon have several in the family. (Rice)

concerned about aggression and think that you will lose your status as "pack leader" with tug-of-war games, do not own a Rottweiler. Rottweilers enjoy physical contact and physical sports, just like some people enjoy football and wrestling. However, tug-of-war or any game with your Rottweiler must be supervised, and *you* must make and enforce the rules.

Another game is the two-hose game. Take two pieces of an old garden hose, approximately one foot long. Wave one of them around a bit to excite your dog, and throw it for him. When he gets it and starts back, wave the second hose and throw it in the opposite direction. Soon you can have your dog running thither and yon dropping a piece of hose near your feet. You get to stand still and your dog gets to run, run and run.

Appropriate toys for a Rottweiler are too-large-to-swallow balls or solid rubber toys, Boomer Balls (large nylon balls), Kongs (beehive shaped rubber toys) and stuffed toys of all descriptions. We recommend that if you choose nylon chew toys that you only purchase the hard nylon, not the soft types, because Rottweilers chew through those soft ones like water and could choke on the pieces. Tires also make great outdoor diversions; just be sure they are not the steel-belted type.

EQUIPMENT YOU'LL NEED FOR YOUR DOG

Crates are a necessity. We will discuss their uses in more detail in Chapter 6. Right now we will just say that there are two types: wire and plastic. Wire

This Rottweiler is safe and relaxed in his wire crate.

crates let the dog see out and you see in. For those fastidious housekeepers, the wire crates also let the dog hair *out*. Plastic crates have solid tops and bottoms with windows on the sides. These are warmer in the winter, hotter in the summer, but they do keep all the dog hair and dirt inside. The choice is yours.

The size of the crate is more important than the type. The crate should be large enough that your dog can stand up and turn around in it. This does not mean standing on his hind legs or even with his head up. A crate that is 30 inches tall, 40 inches long and 20 inches wide is plenty big enough for a large, adult, male Rottweiler. Obviously the crate can and should be smaller for a bitch.

You will probably want some sort of **collar** for your Rottweiler. We recommend that for puppies, you choose a buckle collar that is adjustable. These

Your Rottweiler should always have a collar on when he's outside. (K. Lemley)

The Beenens have their dog Fuzz on a down-stay wearing his training collar and leather leash.

will last until the pup is eight to ten months old, saving you from purchasing a collar a month. Some type of buckle on a collar is mandatory for everyday wear. Buckles allow you to place ID tags and licenses on the dog and also give you a handle to grab if necessary. Choke or slip collars are *never* allowed on your dog unless your dog is attached to you via a leash. Choke collars do just what their name implies. Should your dog catch the live ring of a choke collar on something and struggle against it, he will choke to death.

We recommend only leather leads or **leashes**. Why, you ask? Experience, we reply! Leather is strong and kind to your hands. It is comfortable to hold. We know that leather leads are expensive but think that the expense is well worth it. It is up to you to see to it that your dog does not eat your new, expensive leather leash. Those chain leashes that you see around? Don't use them. They kill your hands if you need to grab a shorter hold on

your dog. The last type leash that is readily available is the nylon type. These come in pretty colors that match your collar and are inexpensive. However, they will melt the fingerprints right off your hands should your dog give a good pull. They are also not nearly so comfortable to hold in your hand because they really do not fold up neatly.

Stainless steel water and food **bowls** are considered the best. They usually last longer, dogs are not as prone to chew on them and they do not break. Perhaps their biggest advantage is that they can be sterilized or at least cleaned more thoroughly than plastic or ceramic dishes.

YOUR ROTTWEILER'S ADOLESCENCE

All Rottweilers go through adolescence. The boys tend to *really* go through adolescence. Since some breeders only have experience with bitches,

Stainless steel bowls may be good for drinking water, but when you really want to get wet, a baby pool is the ticket.

Suppose that you have decided to cut your dog's nails and he begins to grumble about the indignity of having his nails cut. Hear us now: You *must* continue cutting his nails. You're the boss! We have found that arguing over the noise increases the volume. As long as you win the battle of the nails, in this case, leave the griping and complaining alone.

Teenage male Rottweilers, like teenage human males, discover girls. We consider mounting behaviors of humans unacceptable. We also do not think that correcting a dog for inappropriate mounting damages his libido later in life. Mounting children can also be a dominance thing, and that really is *most* unacceptable. When it comes to mounting other canines, stay out of it. The dogs will settle any difficulties themselves, and much more effectively.

we will attempt to give you some pointers for raising a well-mannered, civilized male Rottweiler. You must never encourage or accept growling. Although we can speak Rottweiler and you could someday learn to speak it, most people do not and should not have to learn it.

How to stop growling? Before it gets started. We recommend that you use some type of *extinguishing-of-the-behavior* method. What's that, you ask? We simply mean if the dog growls while being petted, stop petting him. When he is silent you can stroke him.

However, if your Rottweiler decides that he does not want to do something that you have asked him to do and voices his opinion, in this instance he *must* be made to do as commanded.

Lurking inside 15-week-old Lucille is the mind and body of a soon-to-be-restless adolescent.

Neutered dogs and spayed females make great family pets. Stuttgard, Lacy and Storm with Dick and Diane Freebarin.

Males can be a real handful in adolescence. The best way to handle them is to train them consistently and daily.

During this sexual revolution, it is most important that you continue with training classes. You really must stay in charge of your Rottweiler at this time in his life if you are to continue as one big happy family.

DESEXING YOUR ROTTWEILER

Desexing or spaying/neutering your Rottweiler is a viable option for dogs purchased as companion animals. Most reputable breeders will demand that you spay or neuter your pet puppy. Talk to your veterinarian about when your male should be neutered. We recommend spaying your bitch puppy before six months of age. The surgery is far easier before she goes through her first heat cycle. For males, this is an entirely different story.

Males require the testes to achieve secondary sex characteristics. So if you purchased your male pet-quality Rottweiler because you were attracted to the Rottweiler's muscular body and large head, you cannot castrate your Rottweiler before he has developed these characteristics. This will take place by the time he is two to three years of age. This also means that you will have to cope with adolescent behaviors. Should you neuter your male early in his life, he will be a wonderful pet but will grow up to look rather like a bitch. If you don't believe us, just take a look at a steer and a bull or a stallion and a gelding!

Living with Rottweilers has its ups and downs. We hope this book makes for mostly up times. This chapter's helpful hints, along with formal obedience training and advice from your breeder, should make your life with a Rottweiler a joy.

(Chris Carlough)

CHAPTER 6

Keeping Your Rottweiler Happy and Healthy

Assuming that you have done your homework and found a breeder or rescue group from which you will get your puppy or adult Rottweiler, you must now prepare your home for the dog's arrival. You must have the recommended food, a safe and secure place for the new arrival to sleep, toys, leashes, collar and water bowl. You should have also located a veterinarian.

Some vets are not particularly comfortable treating Rottweilers. This is because they have either personally had a bad experience, or one of their colleagues has had a bad experience. You could ask neighbors or other Rottweiler owners to recommend a local veterinarian. If the vet you have chosen acts a bit fearful of your puppy, run, do not walk, to another vet.

YOUR DOG'S DIET

Most breeders and rescue groups will explain diet and give you some food in case you have not located a store that carries the particular brand the dog is currently eating. If you cannot locate a source of this brand, be sure to talk it over with the breeder to see if there is another brand that he or she recommends.

We recommend a quality dry kibble that is not too high in protein (21 to 26 percent is plenty). The kibble you feed should be one that the dog will eat readily, does well on, is convenient to purchase and does not break the household budget to obtain.

The breeder will also explain how often, how much and when the pup has been eating. Most seven- to eight-week-old puppies are given three to four meals per day. As your puppy gets older, the number of meals per day should be reduced. The late-night meal is the first to eliminate from the schedule, then the lunchtime feeding. We recommend feeding Rottweilers twice a day: morning and evening. The meals can be split in half, or you can give a smaller meal for breakfast and a larger meal in the evening. The pup will tell you when to stop the late-night and lunchtime feedings; he will simply lose interest in them. Be sure to gradually increase the amount of food you give as the pup grows.

How much food does a Rottweiler puppy need? The puppy's condition should tell you. A rule of thumb we pass on to our puppy clients is that the pup should gain no more than two pounds per week or ten pounds per month. An obese puppy is one that may develop growth problems, since the bones are not strong enough to support all that fat. He also may not develop his coordination properly because he cannot handle the extra weight. The puppy should have some condition (fat) so that he can survive until he gets back on his paws if he develops some sickness. You should see a waistline as you look down on your pup's back, and you should be able to feel his ribs.

Please remember that the most important nutrient for your Rottweiler is water! Always have cool, fresh water available for your dog. This is especially important in warm weather.

CRATES

Where will your pup or dog sleep? A crate is a good choice. Most breeders will explain the benefits of crates and help you obtain one. Crates are indispensable as far as puppies are concerned. They are safe places for your dog to sleep and spend time when you cannot observe him. If the pup is in his crate, he cannot teeth on your furniture, draperies or, heaven forbid, electrical cords. If he is confined to his crate, he learns to rest when you need him to rest. When he is tired and a bit

Diet is a primary link to good health. Your puppy's breeder should send you home with a quality food, and it's up to you to take over.

Don't let your Rottweiler get fat. Proper diet, exercise and regular weigh-ins at the veterinarian should keep your dog in prime shape.

Crates are not just for housetraining—they also keep your dog safe and secure while traveling.

cranky, it is a safe place away from your children to catch a quick nap. Be sure that the rule of the house, for visitors as well as your own children, is *do not touch the crate or puppy, when crated.*

Crates also make housebreaking a snap. Most dogs will not soil their beds. Thus, a puppy in his crate will try to hold as long as he can, giving you the opportunity to get him to his specified potty area. A distinct potty area is really nice, especially if you do not have an outside kennel run or if the dog shares the yard with children. Insisting that the dog use a particular area means quicker cleanup for you and no land mines for the children. This also makes training the dog to eliminate on command easier. Remember, too, that you cannot housebreak a puppy without going out with him to be sure he

remembered what to do! Just opening the back door is not enough. Pups get outside and start to play and simply forget.

Crates are your dog's den, his safe haven. If you take your new canine family member visiting, you can also take his bed with him, and he will be very secure in his own surroundings. Also, Rottweilers should travel in crates. If he is secured in his crate, sudden stops will not put him through the windshield or other window. Also, should you be in an accident, he cannot escape into traffic, and the paramedics can rescue you if you need assistance. This also makes it easier to pay tolls, get gas and go through drive-through windows at fast food joints.

VETERINARY CARE

The first place your puppy should visit is the veterinarian. The breeder should have given you a shot and worming record when you picked up your pup or rescue dog. Take this record with you on your puppy's first visit to the veterinarian, which should be within 48 to 72 hours. Your vet should perform a general health exam, and after reading the shot record, give you a recommended schedule for inoculations. Be sure to take a fresh stool sample so that the vet can do a fecal exam as well. This exam tells the vet if your dog has internal parasites (and which kinds) so that appropriate wormers can be prescribed. The second most important person in your dog's life is his veterinarian. This first visit is vital to your dog's well-being.

Take your puppy for a general veterinary examination within a few days of getting him.

Heartworm Check

If you are taking a Rottweiler older than six months of age for his first veterinary visit, the vet should pull a blood sample for a heartworm check. Heartworms are very destructive, life-threatening, internal parasites. They are not to be messed with. After testing for heartworm, your vet will make a recommendation of either daily heartworm preventatives or monthly ones. Puppies less than six months old are too young to test, and your vet will probably recommend one of the monthly types of heartworm prevention. As your puppy grows and gains weight, the heartworm preventative dosage must be increased accordingly.

Rottweilers do not have the strongest immune system and are prone to viral and bacterial diseases. You must follow the vet's recommended schedule for inoculations. Your pup should really have had at least three shots for canine parvovirus before you take him to places that other dogs frequent, like the local park or training class.

When you first bring your pup home, while he is young and easily trained to submit, is the time when you must get him familiar with being examined. You must get your puppy used to having his feet picked up and examined, his ear leather lifted, his ears cleaned, his mouth opened, and the like. A fully mature male Rottweiler is not going to appreciate your vet during an emergency if he has not been taught to submit to such examinations. You need to learn to clip nails and brush teeth. These are the two areas most neglected by new owners. The best time to start is when the pup is young.

FLEAS

External parasites are the pits! If you have been doing your puppy homework by regularly examining your pup, you should catch the first signs of flea infestations. Fleas are not to be fooled with because they can and will infest your home and bite people as well as cats and dogs. If you find small, black grains of sand on your Rottweiler, even if you do not see the actual flea, you have a problem. These grains are not sand, but flea excrement. You can bathe your dog in flea soap, dip him or talk to your vet about the new topical flea controls. But you must do it right away! To delay means fogging your house and yard, vet visits, tapeworm treatments and tremendous expense that isn't necessary.

Dogs get tapeworms, an internal parasite, from eating fleas. You will know that your dog has tapeworms because the segments will appear in his stools or even on him. They look like grains of rice when they dry or white, moving, yucky things when adhering to his coat.

If your Rottweilers spend any time outdoors—which they love to do—they should be on a heartworm preventive medicine. (G. Daigle)

Another potential veterinary problem associated with fleas is flea-bite dermatitis. Some dogs are allergic to the flea's saliva and develop an itchy rash when bitten.

Flea bites can also be a cause of a bacterial or fungal infection known as a *hot spot*. Hot spots are very itchy and oozing. If allowed to go untreated, they will spread at an alarming rate and require veterinary attention. If you catch a hot spot early, it is easily treated. First you have to kill the causative agent. Try cleasing the area with Betadine or some other antibacterial soap, and then clip the hair from the area. Cleanse the area again and dry throughly. If the spot does not improve by the next day, consult your veterinarian. After you stop the itching and oozing, you should apply some type of first-aid cream to encourage regrowth of the hair. Do not apply any ointment, however, until the lesions heal. If you make little or no progress with this line of defense, take your Rottweiler to the veterinarian.

Puppies that are used to being handled by all kinds of people won't mind being examined by the veterinarian. (Piusz)

mouth parts near the dog's skin. Firmly pull the tick off the dog and deposit it into a can of rubbing alcohol or gasoline to be disposed of later.

COMMON HEALTH CONCERNS

"An ounce of prevention" is always prudent, especially with curious puppies. Puppies have not had enough life experiences to know what is harmful, so puppy proofing, exactly like child proofing, can prevent accidents.

To begin puppy proofing, examine every inch of your house and yard from the puppies perspective. In other words, get down on your hands and knees and look for poisons, electrical cords, small swallowable objects, and so on, which can be harmful to your puppy (or adult dog). Also be aware of potentially dangerous situations, such as leaving a puppy in a crate with a choke collar or inadequate shade, which can cause heat stress. Taking action to prevent dangerous situations will provide a safe, healthy environment for your puppy and older dog.

TICKS

Ticks are the other external parasite that must be prevented. They are sometimes hard to find on a Rottweiler, but you must do a tick patrol after each walk in the park. Ticks carry some very nasty diseases, like Rocky Mountain Spotted Fever and Lyme disease. It truly is in the best interest of your dog to remove ticks promptly. Do so by numbing the tick with a dab of petroleum jelly or rubbing alcohol. With tweezers, grasp the tick by the

Poisoning

When you think of poisoning, you probably think of someone trying to kill a dog by giving him poison. Though it does happen, most poisonings are accidental—the dog has eaten a toxic plant, ingested a toxic substance such as antifreeze or insecticides or the dog has eaten a whole bar of baker's chocolate. We will not give you specific treatments for poisoning because the treatment is very dependent on the type of poison the dog has

While a life that includes working and playing in the great outdoors can expose your dog to parasites and other harmful critters, they are readily eradicated and shouldn't prevent the dog from doing what he loves.

most plants are poisonous if your dog chews or eats them. Prevention also includes careful reading and following instructions for all medications, flea dips, flea sprays and flea collars you give to or use on your dog.

The second thing we recommend is to purchase the following items and keep them on hand always: syrup of ipecac, hydrogen peroxide, a bottle of activated charcoal (your pharmacist can get it for you) and cotton. Hopefully, you will never have to use them, but, if the need arises, these items can save your dog's life. Do not automatically give them, however, because the treatment will depend on the poison itself. Your veterinarian or the poison control center will tell you how to use them.

The next thing you should do is place your veterinarian's phone number, a 24-hour emergency number and the Poison Control Center number (800-523-2222) by your phone. You will also want to keep a note pad and pen or pencil near the phone.

If you suspect your Rottweiler has been poisoned, call the veterinarian or the Poison Control Center, tell them what you suspect is the cause and write down the treatment you are to administer. If the dog has eaten or chewed a substance in a container, have that container ready to read any needed information from the label.

Linda's friend Jane lost a beautiful puppy once who ate a mushroom. The mushroom happened to be an "Angel of Death," which is very toxic, even

encountered, and the treatments are very different for each poison type. We will give you sage advice, however, based on experience, which could save your Rottweiler's life.

The first thing you should do is take preventative measures. Do not leave any medications (over the counter or prescription), insecticides, candy (especially chocolate), antifreeze, cleaning products, lubricants, and so on, where your dog can get them. Dogs are curious, like to chew and are not particularly finicky about what they will eat. Please remember, too, that all food and medications that are safe for humans are not safe for dogs. Learn the names of all of your houseplants and outdoor plants. It is usually good practice to assume that

This dog has a beautiful coat that's been kept flea and tick free! (Aceti and Hedrick)

in small amounts. Since then, you will not find the Michels or Justice household without the ipecac, peroxide, cotton and, especially, activated charcoal. In case you are wondering about the cotton, it is very useful for swallowed glass or open safety pins. With a coating of peanut butter, dogs will eat a lot of cotton, which will surround the glass or pin, and improves the odds that your dog will pass the object without stomach or intestinal damage.

Choking

Choking can result when your puppy swallows something too large or has "wolfed" down his food, which causes an obstruction of the airway. Choking is a serious, life-threatening condition

and must be dealt with quickly or the puppy or adult dog can suffer brain damage or death in as few as four minutes. The symptoms of choking can vary: a coughing or gagging noise, attempts to expel the object, pawing at the side of the face and, usually, panic. Do not wait until the dog collapses to help him or to get help. Also, DO NOT try to hit the puppy or dog on the back or probe his throat; this may cause the object to move deeper into the airway.

There is a Heimlich maneuver adaptation for dogs. Do become familiar with it before you have an emergency. The approach to assist a choking dog depends on the size of the dog, the cooperation of the dog and the situation. We will give general guidelines.

For Rottweiler puppies (or any small dog): First, push the lower jaw open and tilt the head back. Then, USING EXTREME CAUTION, try to remove the object with your fingers, taking care not to push it deeper. If you cannot easily remove the object, position the puppy for the modified Heimlich maneuver by holding the puppy upright on your lap or placed stomach up on a hard surface with the puppy's hind feet towards you. Place the index finger and middle fingers of both hands on the puppy's abdomen at a point well below the rib cage. Press into the abdomen with a quick, upward thrust. You may need to apply several thrusts to expel the object.

For older Rottweilers (or any large dog): Get another person to assist you if possible. It will be difficult to open a large, panicking dog's mouth, and the struggle could cause the object to move deeper in the airway, so it's best to try the

Always check your dog for ticks when you come back from outdoor excursions.

hard a few times, quickly pressing upward and inward. After successful completion of the Heimlich maneuver, have your dog examined by a veterinarian.

A word of warning about balls is in order here. Linda saw a veterinarian successfully dislodge a tennis ball from a German Shepherd Dog's throat at a dog show, using the Heimlich maneuver. The dog's owner had been throwing ball for the dog, and it went straight down his throat. Sadly, Linda also has a friend who lost her Rottweiler when a hard rubber ball bounced into his throat. Elaine was putting Ludwig into his crate, threw his ball in, and it bounced and went right down his throat. Elaine was unable to dislodge the ball and unable to get Ludwig to the veterinarian in time to save him. Rottweilers do love balls, but remember that balls become very slick with saliva and can slide right into the throat of a large dog.

If your dog has been acting peculiar prior to choking, or if you are not familiar with the choking dog, be careful. In rare cases, this can be a sign of rabies. Take the dog to the veterinarian if you can safely get him transported.

Heimlich maneuver right away. Roll the dog on his back. Place your hands one on top of the other with the heel of the bottom hand on the dog's abdomen below the rib cage. Press into the dog's abdomen with a quick, hard upward thrust and repeat if necessary. You can also try this with the dog on his side, if you can't get him on his back.

If it is difficult to get the dog on his side or his back, you can attempt the maneuver with the dog standing or sitting. Bend over the dog and make a fist with one hand. Place the thumb of your fist against the dog's abdomen below the rib cage. Grasp the fist with your other hand and squeeze

Cardiopulmonary Resuscitation (CPR)

Drowning, accidents and electrical shock are some of the reasons you may need to perform CPR on your dog. The ABC's (Airway, Breathing, Circulation) of CPR can mean the difference between life and death for your dog. However, CPR should not be attempted without knowledge of how to properly administer it. You should not try to learn CPR by practicing on a live animal. Only practice on mannequins because chest compressions, when not necessary, can do harm. We suggest that you enroll in a CPR course for humans and consult your veterinarian about adaptations for dogs. Your local Red Cross chapter can help you find a course. Lori H. Feldman, DVM and Henry J. Feldman, MA EMT-M have an excellent Animal CPR brochure available on the Internet at http://members.aol.com/henryhbk.

Heatstroke

If it were not for the Cass River, Linda's CH. Lindenwood's Bouncer, CD, BH, TT, CGI would not have lived to be 13 years old. In fact, he would not have earned any title nor sired any puppies. When he was 2 years old, he got heatstoke on a cloudy day in September in Frankenmuth, Michigan, about 10 minutes after the dogs had been checked on and given fresh water. It was a humid day, Bouncer was very protective of his crate and van, and he became overheated when passersby looked in the van windows at the dogs. The doors and windows were all wide open and Bouncer was the only dog affected, but he was having difficulty breathing and was hemorrhaging when we came back to the car. Mike Conradt and Bill Michels are both big, strong guys and were able to carry 100+ pounds of unconscious Rottweiler across the street, wade into waist deep water in the river, hold Bouncer's head above water in hopes of getting his body temperature down enough to save his life, while Linda and Debbie Conradt tried to locate the local veterinarian. The

Lynne and Bill Weir lived on a boat with Gale and Toby—who always had lots of fresh water to keep them cool.

river was cold enough to get Bouncer's temperature down, the vet was only a few blocks away and the McDonald's by the vet's office gave us a garbage bag of ice to cool Bouncer down until the vet arrived. Bouncer lived, although it took a good 6 months for him to completely return to normal. We all learned a lesson from this experience.

The symptoms of heatstroke are hard and fast panting, above normal heart rate and bright red mucous membranes. If the dog's body temperature is not quickly returned to normal, the dog will begin to stagger, go into a stupor, will usually have uncontrollable watery diarrhea and start to hemorrhage. Coma and death will soon follow if the dog's body temperature is not lowered quickly.

If you are near a veterinary clinic, take the dog there immediately. If not, get the dog out of the sun or hot area, into the shade or air-conditioning. Immerse his legs and trunk into ice water, Take his temperature at least every 10 minutes and cool him until his temperature reaches 103°F. (It is easy to cool him too much, causing his body temperature to go hypothermic, so stop the cooling when his temperature reaches 103°F [39.4°C].) Continue to monitor his temperature to ensure it does not rise again. When it is stable, take your dog to the veterinarian.

We cannot stress how fast a Rottweiler can develop heatstroke. We know of Rottweilers who have developed heatstroke traveling in a car, especially when stopped in traffic, and when left unattended in an air-conditioned motor home when the power or air conditioner failed. Linda will not leave a dog unattended for more than 5 minutes in the motor home or van with the air-conditioning running. Her one experience with Bouncer will never be forgotten.

This dog needed a cast on his leg—but he recovered. (T. & C. Woodward)

Vomiting

It is not uncommon for a dog to vomit. The design of their stomach and esophagus makes it easy for them to vomit voluntarily with little discomfort. They can vomit when excited, when they've eaten too much, when they've drunk too much water and, especially, when they've eaten a lot of grass. They will also vomit because of motion sickness, which fortunately, most Rottweilers will outgrow.

If your dog has vomited for one of the above reasons, you shouldn't be too alarmed. Keep him away from food and water for a few hours and

gradually reintroduce the food and water. You can give him ice cubes during this time.

If blood is present in the vomit, call your veterinarian immediately. Likewise, if the vomiting persists for any length of time, especially with puppies or old dogs, call your veterinarian.

Diarrhea

Diarrhea can be a symptom of change in diet, overeating, eating rich food or milk, intestinal parasites or a change in water when traveling. It can also be a sign of disease. If the diarrhea is black or green, call your veterinarian immediately.

If the diarrhea is slight and your dog has no other symptoms, keep him away from food for a day, (unless he is a young puppy—then call your veterinarian for advice). Give him a medication such as Pepto-Bismol or Kaopectate every four hours until the diarrhea stops. Consult your veterinarian for proper dosages, but, generally, Pepto-Bismol is given ½ teaspoon per 10 lb. of body weight and Kao-pectate (the kaolin-pectin type) 2 teaspoons per 10 lb. body weight. After 24 hours, begin to reintroduce food in small portions. During this time, makes sure that your dog drinks plenty of water.

Watch your Rottweiler closely for signs of dehydration. To check your Rottweiler for dehydration, pinch the skin over the ribs and pull it up an inch or so. Hold it there for a few seconds and let it go. If your dog is not dehydrated, the skin will spring back quickly and flatten out. If your dog is dehydrated, it will stay there in a little ridge and take 5 or more seconds to flatten out. If your dog is dehydrated or the diarrhea persists, contact your veterinarian.

By paying attention to your dog and his habits, you'll be able to tell if he's not feeling well.

Allergies

Severe allergic reactions require quick care by a veterinarian. Allergic reactions can cause itchy, tearing eyes, sneezing and difficulty breathing. The dog's face may be lumpy and swollen. In a severe reaction, the dog can collapse. If the reaction is severe, get your Rottweiler to a veterinarian as

soon as possible. If it is mild, you can give your dog an antihistamine, such as Benadryl if your dog weighs at least 25 lb. If your dog weighs 25–50 lb., give him 12.5 mg. of Benadryl once a day. If he weighs more than 50 lb., give him 25 mg. once a day. Do not give puppies or pregnant bitches an antihistamine without consulting your veterinarian.

Skunks and Porcupines

If you live in or visit a rural area, your curious Rottweiler can encounter a skunk or porcupine. While these experiences are not usually life-threatening, they are extremely unpleasant for both you and your Rottweiler.

If your Rottweiler has a close encounter with a porcupine, he can have a few quills or many quills, usually on his face. In either case, trying to remove quills yourself will be painful to your dog, and you could be bitten in the process. It is best to have a veterinarian remove the quills, usually under anesthesia.

Skunks usually win encounters with dogs, and the smell of a skunked dog is indescribable. Linda speaks from firsthand experience, a lot of experience unfortunately, and is the local resident expert on "skunkings."

If your Rottweiler is skunked, you won't need to worry about the symptoms, there will be no doubt in your mind when you get a whiff of him. The first thing you should do is put on rubber gloves because the odor will transfer to your hands every time you touch your dog when you're trying to care for him. It does NOT come off. (Linda learned this pearl of wisdom on the evening of her 20th anniversary. She and Bill had had a very romantic dinner, let the dogs out for the last time before a planned romantic evening, and Bouncer encountered a skunk in the compost pile at 11:30 p.m. Not only was any hope of romance killed for the night, but Linda's hands smelled like a skunk for several days afterward, even after scrubbing them until they were raw.) After you are properly gloved, begin care by rinsing your dog's eyes with lukewarm water. Apply a mild antibiotic eye ointment or a few drops of olive oil to ease the discomfort.

More than likely, this will happen at night, and you must try to cut some of the odor so that the dog can come into the house. You cannot get rid of the odor, but you can get some of it out by giving your dog a bath in tomato juice, diluted lemon juice, feminine douche products such as Massengill or a product called Skunk-Off. Skunk-Off can be purchased from a veterinarian or pet supply shop. All will help some and help make the smell tolerable, but none get rid of the odor. It will eventually wear off, but every time your dog gets wet for a few months, it's deja vu with the skunk. Linda's experience with 3 skunkings in 10 years (don't ever have a compost pile near your dog's yard), rates the methods like this: tomato and lemon juice are the least effective and it's a toss-up between Skunk-Off and Massengill douche for the most effective. The best results were with the last skunking when Skunk-Off was used initially, followed by a Massengill bath the following day. That's a pretty powerful statement about Massengill douche products; we don't know why they don't use it in their ads!

There is a potential concern with skunk encounters, however, which will not be evident for a week or so afterward. If the skunk scratches the dog, it can transfer a highly contagious fungal infection, which is easily treated, but no one in the household can touch the dog without gloves for a while. If your dog has sores on his face (or anywhere else) after a skunking, take him to the veterinarian to determine the cause.

This male had a missing tooth and was severely dysplastic. He was neutered and was a wonderful pet for owners Linda and Bill Michels.

The verterinarian should listen to your dogs's heart during regular examinations to ensure activities such as this one can be a part of your dog's life. (J. Owens)

HEALTH RED FLAGS

While your puppy is very young, you must be on guard against viral and bacterial infections. Going off his feed and diarrhea are major causes of alarm. As he gets a bit older, he may develop some lameness. These are also red-flag situations. Some Rottweilers develop growing pains, or panoesteitis. This condition is not life-threatening, but it is a cause for concern. A diagnosis of "pano" can be made by x-ray or even palpation.

A severe limp that does not go away in a few days is a major red flag. Not an emergency, mind you, but you should schedule a vet visit quickly. Front lameness may be due to a tear in the cartilage of a joint. This is known as *osteochondrosis dessecans* or OCD. Sometimes rest will take care of it, other times surgery is required. If your dog develops OCD, you need to talk to your breeder and your vet because some think this condition is genetic and, therefore, you should not breed this animal. The breeder will want to know if it's in his or her line, too.

Hip dysplasia is the condition most people are aware of when it comes to dogs and limping. This condition means that the femur does not fit into the acetabulum correctly (the thigh bone into the hip joint), and arthritis will set in, causing your dog mild to severe pain. X-ray is the only way to make this diagnosis. Hip x-rays are called for when you dog has rear-leg lameness or difficulty getting up. If your dog is less than a year old and shows these symptoms, and you can get a diagnosis, most ethical breeders will replace the pup. Most breeders feel that HD is worsened or brought on quicker by overfeeding puppies. This is another reason to keep your youngster fit and trim.

Rottweilers are also now experiencing heart problems. That initial visit to your vet should most definitely include a careful listening to your dog's heart. Any murmurs detected must be monitored carefully. In most cases, the dogs outgrow murmurs, but there is a condition known as SAS, or *subaortic stenosis,* that is life-shortening. Once again, if your pet is diagnosed with SAS, you must notify your breeder.

Eye problems are known to afflict Rottweilers. The most prevalent is entropion, where the eyelid turns inward. It is most painful for the dog and requires surgery to correct. If left uncorrected, the dog's vision may be in jeopardy because the scratching eyelashes cause corneal ulcers to develop. This condition is universally thought to be genetic, and the affected dog must not be bred. Once again, a call to the breeder is mandated.

Your breeder should have health certificates that certify that the Rottweilers are free of eye diseases, orthopedic conditions, heart problems and thyroid illnesses. Be sure that you see these certificates before buying your puppy.

(Close Encounters of the Furry Kind/J. Harrison)

CHAPTER 7

Caring for Your Rottweiler

You have prepared your home for the arrival of your new canine family member. You have the recommended food, toys, crate, collar and lead. You have taken your dog for his first vet check. Now what? Keep to the schedule the breeder gave you!

Take your pup outside to do his business and stay with him to be sure he does it. Feed your new friend the scheduled amount at the scheduled time. Now it is time to take him back outside to again do his business and perhaps spend some time playing with him.

Feeding and going outside must be kept to a schedule much like a baby's. Eight-week-old pups can hold all night, but it is not fair to expect him to hold longer. If you want to quickly housetrain him, you must stick to a schedule. Crates definitely help, as explained in Chapter 5, "Living with a Rottweiler."

If you must leave your pup unattended because of work, be sure to get a neighbor or family member to come by and exercise and feed your pup his noon meal. This lunchtime break can eventually be eliminated. Gradually increasing the amount of food for breakfast and dinner and gradually extending the time the pup is let outside should get the pup on your schedule without messing up his.

Growing puppies need regular meals along with adequate exercise and rest.

ROTTWEILER ESSENTIALS

Food

Rottweilers need to be fed twice a day for life. A moderate protein diet for the first two years is what we recommend. That is one in which the protein content of the food is 21 to 26 percent. The fat content must be reasonably high (12 to 16 percent) so that the pup has energy to grow and play. After the second birthday, a lower-protein diet should be fed. If your dog is hard at work in obedience, agility, herding or whatever, he might need to stay on the higher-protein food in order to maintain condition. It is not necessary to have him so lean that he looks like a black-and-tan Greyhound, but he should not carry too much extra weight, either. Remember, he should have a waistline and you should be able to feel his ribs.

Exercise

Regarding the amount and kind of exercise for a growing Rottweiler, moderation is always the best answer. Puppies should never be exhausted! Tired, yes, but not to the point of exhaustion. We recommend taking your new pup for slow walks of about 20 minutes duration. Let the pup explore, race around and take quick rests.

You have to take your puppy out to play and take that walk, or he will not give you a minute's peace. If he does not bug you with toys, mouthing your clothing and ankles and untying your shoelaces, he will no doubt entertain himself with your furniture, shoes and other assorted valuables.

As the pup matures, the walks can be of longer duration. Remember this is not a marathon but a leisurely walk so that the pup has time to smell the flowers. Do not forget your plastic baggy for cleanup. Cleaning up after your dog is required in most parks and public areas. This is just part of

Puppies who get in their play and exercise time will be more content and easier to live with. (Justice)

being a responsible dog owner. You do not want to be the cause for the banning of dogs from our parks and beaches. Jogging with your Rottweiler is not recommended until most of his growth is completed; that is at about eighteen months to two years of age.

Most Rottweilers love water and like swimming. This is an excellent way to exercise your dog without stressing growing bones and joints. Remember, moderation! Let the pup find out about the water on his own. If you try to force the issue, you may find that you have scared him off swimming for life. You will have to hose him off if he routinely swims in a chlorinated pool. Be sure that you also pay extra attention to your dog's ears. Ear infections, whether bacterial or fungal, occur more frequently in dogs that swim a lot.

Playing fetch is another way to give your dog some exercise. Retrieving is the basis for herding and most obedience exercises. It is a great way to play, to break up training sessions and to reward a job well done. You should encourage play retrieves while the pup is growing up. Throwing a soft toy a few feet and calling the pup back, then rewarding him with another toy or food treat is all it takes.

Asking your dog to sit and stay for a couple of minutes while on your walk is a good way to get in a little informal training. (J. Owens)

While exercise is important, just spending some quality time with your Rottweiler is what is really required. While on your walks, interject some formal training; talk to him; play fetch; sit down and stroke him; and examine his feet, ears, teeth and so on. Make the most of each minute spent with your dog. Do not think of these exercise times or walks as drudgery. This is the time to establish a real partnership.

CHAPTER 8

Grooming Your Rottweiler

With his relatively short coat, the Rottweiler is a breed that is not too difficult to groom. If you are a picky housekeeper, you will want to brush your Rottweiler fairly frequently, like every other day. Twice each year, your dog will blow his coat. That means shedding. Males tend to have one major shed in the spring, with a lighter one in the fall. Females tend to blow their entire coat with their estrus cycle; that is, they go nearly naked with each heat cycle. When your Rottweiler is shedding, you will want to brush him everyday. It is far easier to brush, comb or rake the dead hair out and gather it up than it is to try to vacuum it up. Rottweilers, with their size and double coat, shed a *lot* of hair.

Equipment needed to do a proper brushing are a *slicker brush* (a device with hundreds of small, curved pins in a rubber base with a handle), a comb to remove the hair from the slicker brush and to comb the dog and some sort of rake or shedding blade. We recommend the Universal Slicker brush, a really good comb like a Greyhound comb and a short-handled rake with two sides—one with widely spaced long teeth on one side and shorter, narrower teeth on the other. You might also want to have a flea comb. That is a comb with very closely spaced teeth that theoretically can comb the flea to the surface. Some breeders recommend a rubber curry. This will be up to you as you groom your dog. Get what works best for you and your canine friend.

TEETH AND NAILS

Teeth and nails tend to be the parts of a Rottweiler's daily grooming that most owners neglect. Dogs do not usually get cavities in their teeth, but they build up tartar at an amazing rate. Tartar causes gum disease in dogs just as in humans. If you start brushing your pup's teeth while he is young, most dogs enjoy it. It is cheaper for you to brush your dog's teeth than to anesthetize him so that your veterinarian can clean the tartar off. Anesthesia is always a risk to your dog's life, and it is an unnecessary risk if you just pay attention and keep your canine's teeth pearly white.

Canine toothbrushes and toothpaste are available in most pet supply stores or at your veterinarian's office. You can also use a human soft-bristle brush and a baking soda–and–water paste as a dentrifice. Some people have used a Water Pik successfully on their dog's teeth. If the tartar should get ahead of you, you can give your Rottweiler a large soup bone that will help loosen tartar as he chews on the bone.

Brushing Teeth

To brush your Rottweiler's teeth, simply hold the brush at a 45-degree angle to the juncture of tooth and gum and brush away. Be sure to do upper and lower jaws and, of course, both sides of his mouth. Do not forget the front teeth (incisors) and fangs (canines), so he has a nice white smile! Clean teeth are important when showing your dog. It is really awful for judges to try to count teeth when they are covered with tartar. Since it is important that Rottweilers have all their teeth, you certainly do not want to have his teeth fall out or have to be pulled because you neglected to keep his teeth and gums healthy.

Clipping Nails

Nails come next. While you need to brush your dog's teeth weekly, toes need attention monthly. Your Rottweiler should walk on the pads of his paws, and you should not hear his nails clicking with each step. You can either cut them, file them, or grind them. The choice is yours and your dog's. Once again, getting your young puppy used to this procedure is most important. Trying to do nails on an adult Rottweiler that has never learned to accept this treatment can be a real thrill!

Brush your Rottweiler's teeth often to keep them clean and white—be sure to use toothpaste specially formulated for dogs.

Several types of nail cutters are on the market. All are good; you just need practice to get used to them. Cutting a black nail is a wee bit tricky but not impossible. Cut off small segments at a time. The first clip should take off rather dry and brittle nail. As you take off more of the nail (remember, just a sliver each time), you will notice the nail material becoming moister and softer. You will also notice a small gray-to-white center. This is the *quick,* or blood supply, and there are nerves in it. If you cut the quick, your dog will protest and the nail may bleed. Keep some styptic powder on hand to stop any bleeding.

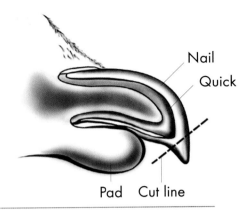

You will not hurt your Rottweiler while cutting his toenails if you don't cut into the quick; if you do, the nail will bleed and your dog will cry.

Keep your Rottie's toenails short enough that you won't hear them clicking on hard surfaces. (Piusz)

Filing your dog's nails is a much longer process. Given the size and strength of Rottweiler nails, this is probably the least successful way to keep his nails short.

Nail grinders are also available. These are motorized, abrasive filing wheels. Some have rechargeable batteries, so you do not need an electric outlet near the dog to use them. If you choose to grind, you have to acclimate your dog to the noise of the motor before you even think about doing his nails. This method takes longer than clipping, but it leaves the nails smoother. You have to go slowly, and you have to go from nail to nail and back again. The friction of the wheel generates heat, and you certainly do not want to annoy your dog by burning his toes.

When you finish doing your dog's nails, be sure to check his ears. They should be clean and pink, with no noticeable odor. Some Rottweilers

Check your dog's ears regularly for wax buildup or infection.

generate a lot of ear wax, and this needs to be removed so that mites or bacterial or fungal infections do not move into this inviting environment. Again, there are lots of ear-cleaning products available at pet supply shops that are effective and easy to use.

BATHING YOUR DOG

How often do you need to bathe your Rottweiler? Whenever he is dirty, smelly or has fleas. If you are brushing your dog frequently, and he does not get to play with other dogs, you will not have to give very many baths. Playing with other dogs tends to give your dog a "doggy odor" and sometimes fleas. But don't deny your Rottweiler this pleasure just because you're lazy about grooming! A well-socialized, but occasionally smelly, Rottweiler is far happier and safer than a too-pampered perfumed pup.

Bathing a Rottweiler is not difficult. Simply wet the dog, apply a canine shampoo, work the shampoo in and rinse thoroughly. In the summer, we give our baths outside with the garden hose. If you bathe your dog in the bathtub, have plenty of towels to dry him or be prepared to wipe down all the walls in the bathroom. If you decide to give a bath when the dog is shedding, it is best to have some sort of screen for the drain of your tub. As stated before, Rottweilers have lots of hair, and it will clog up your drain quickly and effectively.

You may want to bathe your Rottweiler after a particularly dirty day, but otherwise regular brushing should keep him looking and smelling fine. (C. Liebert)

Bathed, dry and ready to show. You'll be proud of your shiny clean Rottweiler after a bath.

After toweling him off, you can use your hair dryer to finish drying him. Dogs do not like to have air blown in their ears, so cover his ears with your hand when drying his neck and head. Brushing the hair as you blow it dry makes the job go faster.

Flea baths are another story. Wet the dog's neck and head thoroughly and apply a coat of flea shampoo around his neck and ears. Fleas have been around for centuries, and they know where to go for safety: in any available orifice, like ears, anus, nose and so on. By applying the shampoo to your dog's neck and ears first, hopefully, the fleas will run to his back and belly, where you will get them next. Then wet the rest of the dog and shampoo. Be sure to leave the shampoo on the dog according to the directions on the bottle. In fact, we recommend leaving the shampoo on a bit longer to

be sure the fleas are killed and not merely stunned. Rinse thoroughly afterward. Blow drying and brushing are recommended to be sure the dead and dying fleas are off the dog.

Dry Baths

For quick cleanups, especially in the cold months, you can use any of several types of dry baths. These are products designed to clean the dog's coat without the need for shampoo and water. Some are foams. Some are pump sprays. Just follow the directions on the product. While they do not do as good a job as a real bath, they certainly help remove the dust and grime quickly and with less hassle than a bath.

Don't forget to wipe away excretions from the eye with a soft cloth or tissue.

(Vicky Cook)

CHAPTER 9

Showing Your Rottweiler

Dog shows began as a way to showcase breeding stock. It was a way to measure the quality of one's kennel. It was a rich man's hobby. Things are slightly different today because the era of the huge breeding kennels is over. Today rich and poor, young and old match their dogs together to either measure the quality of breeding stock or to amass wins. Some affluent owners strive for number one this or that. Some dedicated breeders strive to improve their stock. It really makes no difference the reason, dog shows are fun.

Dog shows can be family affairs, with children in junior showmanship and adults in obedience and conformation classes. There is always plenty to watch and lots of interesting people to meet. The sport of purebred dogs can be played on many levels. It is up to you and your dog at which level you play.

The very first step to take is to go to a dog show. You need to attend a couple of shows just to see what is happening. Even if you have never been to a show but have purchased a show prospect, the first thing to do is to go to shows. Leave your pup at home, wander around, watch, listen and learn all you can. If at all possible, attend a specialty show; an independent specialty is the best. A specialty show has larger Rottweiler entries, and an independent specialty has Rottweilers only and usually means several days of Rottweilers only.

LEARNING TO SHOW

Once you have that potential show dog, the next step is teaching the pup how to show. Most kennel clubs offer handling classes. Taking your pup to these classes accustoms him to stacking in a show pose, being examined by strangers and gaiting properly. These classes also teach you how to stack or pose your pup, bait him for expression and gait or move him correctly. They are also a great place to meet new friends and learn about all kinds of breeds. It will be these friends from handling class that cheer you on or commiserate your losses.

Depending on the size of the show, there are hundreds to thousands of entries and only a few winners. Remember that most people lose at dog shows. So prepare yourself for

Talk to your dog's breeder about getting involved in showing and which shows are best to start out in. (George Shagauwat)

When pups strike poses like this, breeders believe they're destined for the show ring.

losing, since that is what you will do most often. The few times you win will keep you coming back for more. One of the reasons we urge you to work with your dog is so that when you are discouraged by the breed ring, you have another avenue to explore. There are more "winners" in performance events because earning a qualifying ribbon is most satisfying.

To continue your education in showing dogs, your second major source of knowledge, skill and encouragement will be your breeder. Your breeder will know when to show your pup and under which judges. He or she will show you how to fill out entry forms and help you get on a show superintendent's mailing list. Show superintendents produce premium lists. It is these premium lists and, of course, the AKC Calendar of Events that will tell you when and where the show will be held, who is judging, the closing date for entries and the cost of the entries.

ENTERING A SHOW

Once you have made an entry, the superintendent or show secretary will send you an acknowledgment a few days before the show. This acknowledgment is called a *judging schedule*. The judging schedule includes directions to the show, hotels and motels near the show site and, of course, a complete schedule of entries. You will learn your catalog number, as well as what time and in which ring your Rottweiler will be shown.

We are getting just a bit ahead of ourselves, so let's go back. If you are still eager for more knowledge, there are numerous books and videos available. Handling seminars are also offered for kennel clubs by top professional handlers. If the opportunity arises, attend a show with the breeder or one of your handling classmates as his or her groom. This will give you first-hand experience in what to take, how to pack for yourself and your dog, what equipment is needed, how to prepare and groom the dog and yourself and so on.

You now have a reasonably trained puppy, some show experiences and your bait. It is time to try your hand at this new game, so go to a match. A *match* is a pretend dog show. Everything is done at a match like it is done at a show, but wins carry no AKC championship points. Matches are for puppies to teach them all about being show dogs, they are for judges to teach them about various

Handling seminars and classes can teach you how to stack your dog in the ring, and many other helpful tips.

breeds and give them experience judging them, and they are for green handlers to give them experience.

Besides gaining experience for yourself and your puppy, once again, you will meet new friends.

MAKING GREAT BAIT

One of the first lessons that must be learned for successful handling is preparing bait. *Bait* is the term used for the food treats given to the dog in the ring to help him show better. Here is our secret recipe for dog show bait.

If possible, purchase fresh liver. Pork liver is the best, but beef liver will do. Chicken liver should be used only as a very last resort. It is also best to get a lobe of liver and slice it yourself. Presliced, frozen beef liver is fine if that is the best you can find.

Okay, you have the liver. Now what? Thaw the liver if necessary. After thawing, place the liver in a large pan of cold water and soak for 30 minutes to an hour. Change the water several times. This cold-water soak helps remove the blood from the liver.

Change the water one last time and add lots of salt and a couple of dashes of garlic powder. Cover the salt water, garlic and liver and bring to a boil. Reduce the heat and let the pot simmer for 20 minutes.

After 20 minutes of simmering, remove from heat and immediately wash each piece of liver in cold, running water. You can either air dry or place the boiled-and-rinsed liver in the microwave. If you choose to dry the bait by microwave, sprinkle with a little more garlic powder. Nuke the liver on medium for one or two minutes.

Our most important secret comes with storing the boiled-and-dry liver. You must store your newly cooked bait in *paper*. Any brown paper bag will work well. Storing in a brown bag will allow the liver to further dry. It can be kept this way for several days. You now have nice, dry liver that can be carried in the pockets of good clothes without fear of ruining them. Do not seal the liver tightly in plastic bags because it will become slimy and turn green.

These friends do not all have to be Rottweiler owners; the more you learn about dogs in general, the better your life will be with your Rottweiler.

Remember what was said previously about losing? Well, when you lose at a dog show, the day can have a happy ending if your friend wins in another breed. Also, these new friends may make future traveling companions. Going off for a weekend or circuit of shows gets to be expensive, so having a traveling companion cuts the costs down to bearable.

THE BIG SHOW

"Are you ready for some football?" Are you ready for a real dog show? After attending several matches, perhaps you are ready, but only if your pup is winning or placing high in his class. There is really no sense in making entries; driving several hundred miles; and paying for meals, motels and other expenses if your pup is not ready for the big time. Some pups may never be winners as puppies but may mature into quite handsome adults. Your

If you have a young or inexperienced dog, or you need practice yourself, enter a match show.

You'll make real friends showing your dog—who else would put up with conditions like these?

breeder should be honest with you and help you achieve success. No need to burn you out just because your dog is not ready.

Well, the time is quickly approaching for puppy's debut—what to do, what to expect? If you have been going to the matches and attending shows, you will have a pretty good idea. The first thing is to make your entries in a timely manner. If the show offers a puppy sweepstakes, be sure to mark that class in the box for additional classes. Sweepstakes are for fun. They are usually judged by breeders and are basically another arena in which to give your pup some show experience. Since the prizes are a percentage of the entries, a big sweeps win can pay for part of your trip.

Between matches and sweeps, you should, by now, have a fair knowledge of ring procedures and what to do and expect on show day. We always recommend arriving early so there is plenty of time to find a parking space, potty both you and your dog, buy a catalog and settle in. Catalogs are the play book for dog shows. They include all the pertinent information about the dogs entered in the show and list the entries in each class for each breed.

Watching and Waiting

Plan on getting to ringside early so that you have an opportunity to observe the judge's ring procedures. Judges do not usually change their methods, so the way the Dobermans are judged and gaited is more than likely the way the Rottweilers will be judged and gaited. The time to approach the ring

"Are we ready for the real thing?"

you are the only entry, the judge may request that you gait around the ring before stacking. This is a time-saving measure on the part of the judge; if your dog is lame, you are excused immediately, and the judge does not take the time to examine your dog.

That first brief look and once-around are very important, so look your very best. That first impression made on the judge's mind will have a lot to do with his or her final selections and placements. When the dog ahead of you is being gaited, move into position and stack your dog. Nothing annoys a judge more than having to wait for a dog to be posed. Judges are on strict time schedules, so be ready!

The judge should turn around after watching the previous dog gait to the end of the line and find your pup all stacked and looking marvelous. The judge then moves to the front to

steward to ask for your armband is when he or she is not busy calling a class or marking absentees. Your armband number will match the catalog number of your dog. Place the armband on your left arm.

YOUR TURN IN THE RING

The steward will call your class, and you will enter the ring, usually by catalog number. Both the steward and the judge will check you in, so be prepared to show your armband. Once you are checked in, begin to stack your dog. The judge usually takes a brief look at the entire class posed and then moves the entire class once or twice around the ring. If

Go to the ring early to observe another class in action.

The first impression you make on the judge is a lasting one: Make it good!

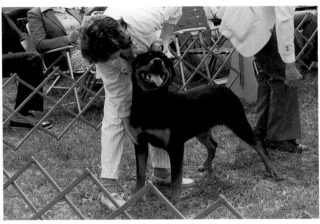

This dog is ready to have his mouth examined!

assess your dog's head and expression and then moves in for a closer inspection of bite and dentition. When the judge asks for bite, hold the collar with two fingers of your right hand under the dog's chin and raise the dog's head so the judge can see. With the thumb and forefinger of your left hand, raise the lips, and with the thumb and forefinger of your right hand, lower the flews. This gives the judge a clear view of your dog's bite (as long as your head is not in the way). At a dog show, you are showing the bite to the judge— you do not need to bend over and look at it too!! You should be very familiar with your dog's bite from practicing at home.

Once the judge is satisfied with your dog's bite, he or she needs to count your pup's teeth. Remember that the standard says that two or more missing teeth are a disqualification. There are several ways to show your dog's dentition. One way is to lift the lips on each side and then open the mouth so the molars can be counted. A second

method is to pull the lips back and open the mouth so that all teeth are exposed at one time. Practice determines which method works for you.

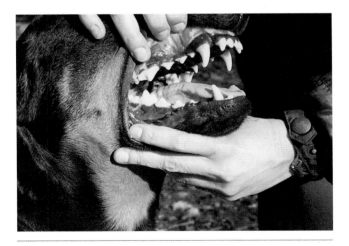

Your Rottweiler must be taught to readily and willingly show his teeth to the judge.

After the mouth is examined, the judge continues to examine the rest of your dog's body. As the judge moves backward, be sure to hold your pup by the muzzle. This assures the judge that you know what you are doing and are prepared to prevent any aggressive moves on the part of your dog. This also is a signal to your dog that he is to accept this examination without complaint. Any attack or attempt to attack is grounds for immediate and permanent disqualification. After spending all this time, money and effort, you surely do not want to get your pup DQ-ed.

When the judge turns to your dog, this should be the first thing he or she sees: a stacked and ready Rottweiler. (Lee Whittier)

It does not matter which pattern is asked for—the important things to remember are to go in straight lines and to stop and pose your dog without running over the judge. After this final look, you will be asked to gait around the ring to the back of the line of dogs. At this time, if the class is large enough, you should let your pup rest.

Keep an eye on the judge so that when the last dog in line is being gaited, you are now stacking and getting your dog's attention. The judge will come down the line of dogs making a final inspection. He may ask for more movement, he may make a *cut* (that is, keep some dogs and excuse others from further consideration) or he may just place the class. Be ready. If that judge points to you, whoopee! But you have to be alert because some judges nod or point just once and then go on. Don't miss your chance.

Gaiting Your Dog

After examining your pup's body parts, the judge asks you to move him so that the way he moves can be assessed. This individual gaiting is usually done in one of two ways: straight away from the judge and straight back to him, known as *down and back,* or in a path that forms a triangle. If it is to be a triangle, the judge asks you to go down one side of the ring, across the back of the ring and then diagonally back to him.

PROFESSIONAL HANDLERS

All this discussion has been about you showing your own dog. If this is not your cup of tea, do not

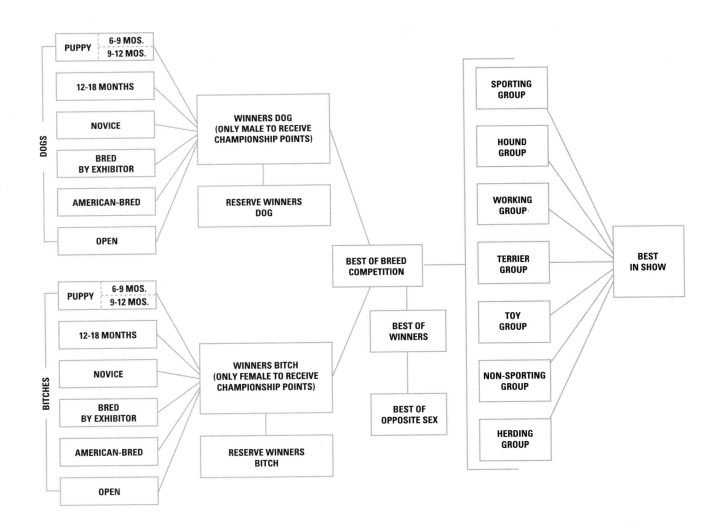

A dog finishing his gaiting pattern in the ring.

the *Professional Handlers Guild* (PHG). If handlers have been certified, they will have a pin that states that they are a *certified professional handler* (CPH). Handlers charge a fee for showing your dog in each class. They also charge you travel expenses and board if they carry the dog to the shows. Be sure that you know what will and will not be charged; this ensures that there will be no need to fire a handler because you became angry over a handling bill.

The handler does not have to transport your dog. You can be what is referred to as a *ringside pickup.* This means that you take the dog to the show, and the handler simply gets the dog at ringside, shows him and hands him back to you. This is the cheapest way in terms of handler expenses, but you have to drive, stay in a motel, eat in restaurants

despair of dog shows. Your breeder may handle for you, or you can hire a professional handler. Either of these options, though, does not free you from handling classes and matches. The training process is still up to you.

Should you decide to hire a handler, ask your breeder for suggestions. When you are attending those first few shows without your dog, watch the handlers. Their names are listed as agents in the catalog. Speak to them and ask their availability. Be sure to go to their setup, see how the dogs are cared for and get a rate card. If you are going to trust your dog to their care, you really need to know all about them.

Two professional handler organizations inspect and certify handlers: the *Professional Handlers Association* (PHA) and

If you're not comfortable showing your Rottweiler, you can hire a professional handler.

Even if you hire a handler to show your dog, you may still be responsible for getting him ready and bringing him to the show. (Maisar)

Your dogs won't change because they won or lost at the show. They'll still think you're the greatest and look to you to take good care of them.

and incur other such expenses. It sometimes really is cheaper to let a handler transport your dog to multishow circuits. Just be sure that you really trust that handler.

BEAR IN MIND

Here are some final words of advice: Your dog does not change because he won or lost at a dog show, and your life does not change because you won or lost at a dog show. Your Rottweiler remains your best canine friend and still deserves your respect and devotion. You still have to go to work on Monday morning and love and support your spouse and children. Do not let dog show wins affect your life. You really are not a better human being because your dog won something or the other. We wish you the best of luck. We hope to meet you at some future dog show, but most of all, we hope you have fun!

(Thora Thibaut)

CHAPTER 10

Obedience Trials, Performance Events and Other Activities for Your Rottweiler

Because of the Rottweiler's multipurpose background, he can and does excel in a variety of performance events. One of the easiest titles a Rottweiler can earn is the *Canine Good Citizen* (CGC) offered by the AKC. This program merely requires the dog to demonstrate his good manners. During the CGC test, your Rottweiler will be asked to walk nicely on a loose lead. He must also allow a friendly stranger to approach the two of you and allow a stranger to groom him. He must remain under control during distractions by a jogger or another dog. The last test is for your Rottweiler to stay quietly for five minutes with you out of his sight. This last exercise is really a supervised tie-out: The tester stays near the dog, who is tied to a tree or post.

OBEDIENCE

The American Kennel Club offers Rottweilers the opportunity to earn titles in obedience, tracking, agility and herding. The Rottweiler does very well in obedience, especially now that more inducive training methods are used. Inducing methods include food, toys or clickers to direct dogs to the desired response, making the training much more fun for dog and handler than the compulsive methods that use negative stimuli, such as collar jerks, to get the dog to avoid displeasure by performing an exercise correctly.

The highest AKC Obedience title is the *Obedience Trial Champion* (OTCH). There are

currently eleven Rottweiler Obedience Trial Champions; these dogs are listed in Chapter 11, "Headliners." Each year, Rottweilers earn more than 400 AKC Obedience titles.

Obedience is a three-tiered program offering the *Companion Dog* (CD), the *Companion Dog Excellent* (CDX) and the *Utility Dog* (UD) titles. There are also advanced titles for dogs with a UD: the *Utility Dog Excellent* (UDX) and *Obedience Trial Champion* (OTCH). To earn a Companion Dog title, the dog and handler team must qualify three times under three different judges in the Novice class at AKC-licensed trials. A qualifying score is earned if the dog passes all the exercises, achieving a score of 170 out of 200. The dog and handler must show teamwork, willingness and enjoyment on the part of the dog and naturalness on the part of the handler while they perform heeling on and off leash, a stand for examination, coming when called and stay in a sit position for one minute and a down for three minutes.

The CDX title builds on the skills learned at the Novice or CD level and adds some new exercises. In the Open class at licensed trials, the dog/handler team performs a heel off leash, stopping and lying down when called, two retrieves (one of them over a jump), a broad jump and staying in place while the handler leaves the ring. The stays are of longer duration: The sit is three minutes and the down is five minutes. Both are done with the handler out of sight of the dog.

In the Utility class, where dogs compete for the UD title, the first test is called the *signal exercise*. The dog heels off leash and demonstrates distance control by standing, lying down, sitting and

Staying in the long sit with the handler out of sight is one of the exercises required in Open obedience.

Chloe shows willingness and enjoyment while she heels off-lead, a team performance.

Lizzie is doing the scent discrimination exercise that's part of the Utility class.

coming on the hand signals of the handler. The next exercise is *scent discrimination,* when the handler provides ten articles—five made of leather and five made of metal. The judge selects one of each and places them near the handler. The steward takes the other eight, handling each one and placing them in a random pile about twenty feet from the dog. The handler then takes one of the judge's articles and holds it in his hands for a short time. The judge takes the handler-scented article and places it in the pile. The handler gives his scent to the dog and sends the dog to the pile to find and retrieve the handler's article. This is done for both leather and metal articles.

The *directed retrieve* follows scent work. Three cotton gloves are placed in the ring while the dog and handler face away from the gloves. On the command of the judge, the handler turns around, points to the correct glove and sends the dog to retrieve it. In the next exercise, the handler moves forward with the dog and signals a stand-stay while

CH Nordike Brinka v. Gruppstark, A/C, CDX, BH, HIC, TT, CGC, TDI, sails over the high jump. (Fot-A-Pet)

The dog must place first three times, once in Open, and once in Utility, plus earn a third first-place win. He must accumulate 100 points by either winning or placing second in either Open or Utility. The points earned depend on the number of dogs competing in each class.

Obedience is fun and demanding. You can work very hard and earn high scores and class placements. But there is also room for those who do not have the time or talent for high scores. You only have to qualify three times to earn an Obedience title.

continuing forward. The judge then approaches and examines the dog, as in the Conformation ring. The last Utility exercise is *directed jumping*. A solid and a bar jump are located on the sides of the ring. The dog is sent away from the handler between the jumps until the handler stops and sits the dog. The judge then tells the handler which jump to send the dog over. This process is repeated for both jumps.

Once a dog has achieved the Utility Dog title, he is eligible to try for the *Utility Dog Excellent* (UDX) and the *Obedience Trial Championship* (OTCH) titles. To earn the UDX, the dog must qualify in both the Open and Utility class on the same day, and he must do this at ten shows. Earning the OTCH is a bit more complicated.

TRACKING

For those who would rather be outdoors and do not mind early-morning walks, perhaps tracking is your dog sport. You can earn a *Tracking*

Tracking involves the dog following a scent over a course of some distance. . .

Dog (TD) title by having the dog follow an hour-old human track for about 500 yards and find the track layer's lost glove. If you and your dog really enjoy this, you can try for the *Tracking Dog Excellent* (TDX) title. This involves a 1,000-yard track, aged three to five hours, and finding several articles along the way. If you really want a challenge, you can attempt the *Variable Surface Tracker* (VST) title, which follows a track layer over concrete, macadam or gravel. If you earn all three tracking titles, your dog is considered a *Champion Tracker* (CT). Tracking is one of the most rewarding and thrilling of the performance events. You cannot force a dog to scent, so it is truly a working partnership with your canine friend.

. . .and finding the "article" that marks the end (in this case a glove).

AGILITY

Probably the most exciting performance event is agility. It is a sport that is literally growing by leaps and bounds. Again, it is a three-tiered sport, with Novice (NA), Open (OA) and Excellent (AX) divisions that require three qualifying scores for the titles. As the levels go up, so do the number of obstacles, as well as the speed and required control of the dog. Agility involves the dog successfully completing each obstacle in a set time. In Novice, there are ten to twelve obstacles; in Open there are fifteen obstacles; in Excellent, there are more than twenty. There are jumps, see-saws, A-frames, weave poles, tunnels and a raised walk. The see-saw, A-frame and dog walk are considered contact equipment, and the dog must step in the yellow-painted areas at each end in order to qualify. All jumps must be cleared, and no knockdowns are allowed. If your dog successfully qualifies in the Excellent class ten times, he earns a *Master Agility* (MX) title.

A typical agility course includes all kinds of obstacles the dogs must negotiate while they are timed.

Training a Rottweiler over the see-saw.

Agility has become so popular a new class was added that only involves weave poles (shown) and jumps.

There is so much enthusiasm for the agility sport that the AKC began offering more titles in the spring of 1998. These titles are called *Jumpers with Weaves,* and the classes contain only jumps and weave poles. Without the contact equipment, these classes are very, very fast. The titles are the same as in regular Agility: Novice (NAJ), Open (ONJ), Excellent (AXJ) and Master (MXJ), but the abbreviations have added a "J" to indicate "Jumpers with Weaves."

If you are a bit of an athlete and your dog has good jumping skills, plus is able to take direction, agility just might be your cup of tea. It is a great workout for you and your dog, so both of you need to be in reasonable physical condition. Most obedience clubs also offer agility classes. If you are interested, be sure to ask if agility is offered at your training class or if there are classes nearby.

HERDING

The last American Kennel Club activity in which Rottweilers can earn titles is herding. It is quite thrilling to see the ages-old instincts come shining through. A dog really cannot be taught how to herd; he must have the innate instincts to gather the herd/flock and bring it to you. Herding titles are a bit different than the other performance events, in that there are Test-level titles, requiring two passing scores, and Trial-level titles, requiring three qualifying scores. The Test-level titles are *Herding Tested* (HT) and *Pretrial Tested* (PT). These

Rottweilers have an innate instinct to herd, which is reinforced by training. (McDowell)

classes show the dog's instincts with some control. The Trial-level classes require lots of control over the dog, and the flock/herd is moved about a set course.

If you want to give herding a go, there are clinics available as well as non-AKC instinct tests throughout the country. *Herding Instinct Certified* (HIC) and *Herding Capability Tested* (HCT) are two such tests. These tests will give you an idea of your dog's talents. They will also provide you with friends and possible training classes.

The American Kennel Club is not the only organization that offers performance titles in the United States. The United Kennel Club offers Obedience and Agility titles similar to those of the AKC. Naturally, the rules are slightly different, but they include the same three levels, with three qualifying scores. There are at least two other dog-agility organizations that offer titles: the *North*

American Dog Agility Club (NADAC) and *United States Dog Agility Association* (USDAA). Each has it owns rules and jump heights.

As previously mentioned, there are also other herding organizations. The *Australian Shepherd Club of America* (ASCA) offers both obedience and herding. The *American Herding Breeds Association* (AHBA) offers instinct tests and Trial-level titles.

OTHER FUN EVENTS

Carting, draft work or weight pulling are other types of events you and your Rottweiler might enjoy. A cart and harness is all you need—that and a willing canine partner.

Flyball is a team sport that most ball-crazy Rottweilers take to. This is a relay race where each dog, on a team of four dogs, races over four hurdles, ten feet apart, catches a tennis ball and races back

Rottweilers are naturals at pulling carts, sleighs and other heavy loads. Jan Marshall is pictured here.

over the hurdles. As each team member completes the course, the next dog starts. The fastest team wins.

THERAPY WORK

If you are not that athletic or training classes are too far away, you and your Rottweiler might try therapy work. All communities have rest homes and hospitals. You and your dog can provide valuable assistance to the patients residing in these institutions. No special training is required, just patience, gentleness and the ability to share love and affection. Some Rottweilers have gotten so good at this service that they are used in physical therapy to help patients regain coordination.

Flyball is great fun for dogs who live to race and retrieve tennis balls. (J. Justice)

SCHUTZHUND

The Rottweiler also does well in the European dog sport of schutzhund. This sport requires the dog to excel in tracking, obedience and protection work. A calm, confident and courageous dog is needed for these events.

The dog must pass a preliminary test for steadiness before being allowed to compete on the schutzhund field to earn a Schutzhund I title. This is called *Begleithund* (BH).

There are three levels of titles: Schutzhund I, II and III (SchH I, II, III). To earn a Schutzhund I, II or III title, your dog must pass all three test phases (tracking, obedience and protection) at the same trial. The tracking phase requires the Rottweiler to use his scenting ability to track over different terrain and through varied vegetation. The dog must change direction, follow the track accurately and with commitment, find articles dropped by the tracklayer and indicate them to the handler.

In the obedience phase, the exercises done by the dog and handler team are similar to AKC Open and Utility exercises, except they are performed on a trial field similar in size to a soccer field. The Rottweiler must heel on and off lead and must sit, down and stand on command while the dog and handler are moving. There is a dumbbell retrieve similar to AKC trials, but in addition, the Rottweiler must retrieve over a one-meter-high jump and over a six-foot scaling wall. Schutzhund obedience also includes a down-stay and a long send-away exercise.

All three tests are demanding of the dog and handler, but it is the protection phase that best shows the relationship between dog and handler

Schutzhund is a European dog sport that combines training obedience and protection work to make an all-around dog.

This is a Schutzhund retrieve over an A-frame exercise.

and demonstrates tremendous control by the Rottweiler. The Rottweiler must search six blinds in sequence to find the trial helper, who acts as the "bad guy." Even though the Rottweiler thinks he knows which blind holds the helper, he still must search each one until finding him. The Rottweiler cannot attack the trial helper unless he or the handler is attacked. When either dog or handler is attacked, the Rottweiler must, without hesitation, launch a full attack—biting only the protective sleeve worn by the trial helper. When commanded by the handler to "out," the Rottweiler must release his catch immediately.

The properly trained Schutzhund Rottweiler must never be aggressive except in those situations for which he is trained and, even in those situations, is always under the absolute control of the handler. Schutzhund protection is often misunderstood by the general public. If you confuse a schutzhund-trained dog with an "attack dog," please take the time to learn about the sport—especially that the rigorous training and control involved in the tracking, obedience and protection work does not produce dogs who attack randomly. We trust trained Schutzhund dogs far more than the average untrained dog of any breed, who does not have life experiences that teach him control and discretion in strange situations.

Schutzhund also offers a tracking title, *Fahrtenhund* (FH), and an endurance title (AD). Finding quality trainers is probably one of the most difficult parts of this sport. Three associations offer titles in schutzhund in the United States: the *United States Rottweiler Club* (USRC), the *United Schutzhund Clubs of America* (USA) and the

CH Winterhawk's Chief Justice, UDT, SchH I, has found the "bad guy" behind a blind.

American Landesverband of the *Deutscher Verband der Gebrauchshundsportvereine* (DVG).

SEARCH AND RESCUE

For the real outdoors type with a willing and able canine partner, there is search and rescue work. This is usually done with a volunteer organization that trains dog and handler in search and rescue operations. Training involves map reading, radio communications and first-aid techniques for the handler, and tracking and air-scenting skills for the dog to master. *Search and Rescue* (SAR) teams must be ready at the drop of a hat to jump in their vehicle and go on a search for up to three days. SAR teams assist local law enforcement in finding lost children and adults. They also help locate bodies on land or in water. The most famous SAR teams are those that worked the Oklahoma City bombing site or assist at earthquake and landslide locations around the world.

The Rottweiler is a very versatile worker. He has done almost any job imaginable for mankind, and he has done that job extremely well. Law enforcement agencies have used Rottweilers for

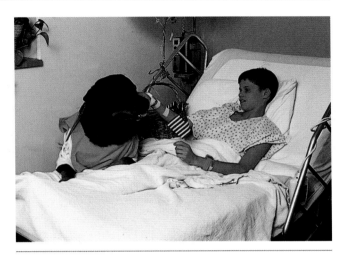

Some Rottweilers simply excel as therapy dogs, one of their many roles as a versatile, devoted working dog. (Rice)

narcotics, bomb and arson detection. The police and military have used them for patrol duty and as perimeter guards. The blind have used Rottweilers for guide dogs, and people with disabilities have used them for assistance work. All this—in addition to the Rottweiler's main tasks as a family companion, herder and guardian dog—really makes him a service to humankind.

(Photos by Mitchell)

CHAPTER 11

Headliners

This chapter is perhaps the most difficult for two people to write because each of us has our own ideas of what makes a dog great. The first time Cathy saw CH Erno Von Wellesweiler, SchH I, she knew that she had seen a real Rottweiler. It has been this image, remembered from the Philadelphia Kennel Club show in December 1969, that has given her breeding program direction. When International CH Cendy Von Seidlerpfad, SchH III, was shown to Best of Opposite Sex at the 1987 ARC Nationals, Cathy knew she had just seen a truly great Rottweiler bitch. Neither of these Rottweilers was a great winner in terms of Best in Show, nor were they great producers in terms of dozens of champions, but Cathy will never forget them.

Linda, on the other hand, saw and met the bitch CH Northwind's Indigo, CD, TD, SchH I; and it is because of her tremendous character and trainability that the Michels' got into Rottweilers and began schutzhund training. The first male Rottweiler that made Linda stop and do a double take was the Best in Show–winning CH Oscar vh Brabantpark. Are these two Rottweilers better than Cathy's picks? The point is a moot one. It makes no difference: All four were important for no other reason than that they influenced two breeding programs.

V-2 CH West Winds Blitz un Donner, CDTD, HT, CGC, TT, with owner Darren Bobrosky. (Roger LeMar)

We suppose that most folks think of headliners as the dogs with the most Bests in Show or some other type of show record. Certainly, some of these top show dogs have also proven to be top sires and dams. We have included the American Rottweiler Club's list of Gold producers in Appendix D, "The Hall of Fame American Rottweiler Club Production Awards." These are the Rottweiler dogs and bitches who have proven themselves through their offspring. In order to achieve this distinction, the sires and dams must not only produce champions of record but also advanced working titlists. These are the Rottweiler headliners that make the future. One of them is pictured on page 102—Int'l/Am/Can/Mex CH Quick Von Siegerhaus, CDX, ZtPr, SchH I, Top 10 *Kennel Review* Top Producer, ARC Gold Producer.

With every puppy, there's new potential. (T. & C. Woodward)

The dog with the record for the most all-breed Best in Show wins is also an ARC Gold Sire. He is three-time National Specialty Best of Breed winner CH Cannon River Oil Tanker, CD, bred and owned by Elfie Rice of the state of

Gold Sire Belgian CH Grave Kapenborgh, SchH I, CD.

Washington. Some 60 Rottweilers have won all-breed Bests in Show, so we will not name all of them.

If you are truly interested in the current top 20 conformation Rottweilers or any of the top 10 performance dogs, you will find them on the American Rottweiler Club's Web site at www.amrottclub.org.

We include here a list of American Kennel Club firsts. These are dogs who are stars simply by being the first to achieve some American Kennel Club award.

ROTTWEILER FIRSTS

The first AKC-titled Rottweiler was Gero V. Rabenhorst, owned and trained by Arthur Alfred Eichler of Wisconsin. He earned his Companion Dog (CD) title in 1939, his Companion Dog

Best in Show and Top-Ten Dog, also a Gold Sire, Am/Can CH Haakon Moby von Reishoff.

Excellent (CDX) title in 1940 and his Utility Dog (UD) title in 1941. It took 27 years for a second Rottweiler to earn a UD.

The first AKC champions of record were recorded in January 1949. They were littermates CH Zero, owned by Noel Paul Jones of California, and CH Zola, owned by Erna Pinkerton, also of California. Zero and Zola's pedigrees can be traced back to the first AKC-registered litter, the Wellwood "A" litter.

Other "firsts" for our breed in AKC events follow:

- The first Rottweiler to win a Group was CH Rodsden's Kurt VD Harque.

- The first all-breed Best in Show Rottweiler was A/C CH Rodsden's Kato v Donnaj, CDX, TD (1971). His full brother, A/C CH Rodsden's Duke du Trier, was the second on the very next day.

- The first Rottweiler bitch to win an all-breed Best in Show was breeder/owner Sheryl Hedrick's CH Pioneer's Beguiled.

- The first CH-UD was CH Don Juan, UD, owned and trained by Margareta McIntyre in 1968.

- The first CH-UDT was Jim and Edna Woodward's CH Axel v.d. Taverne, UDT.

- The first AKC tracking–titled Rottweiler was Russell's Herzchen; the result was published in January 1970.

- The first AKC Tracking Dog Excellent was the DeVinney's Barsoom's Dejah Thoris in 1980.

- The first AKC CH-UDTX was either CH Rodsden's Frugl V Brabant, UDTX, or CH Von Bruka Flying High, UDTX. Both results were published in January of 1984.

- The first AKC CH TDX was Mrs. Don Hardin's CH Rodsden's Anna Feeka Brabant, TDX, in October 1982.

Not the first Rottweiler to earn a TDX, but an impressive record-holder nonetheless is Von Gailingen's Mike Hammer, A/C UD, TDX.

- The first AKC Obedience Trial Champion was George Beck's OTCH Mondberg's Donnamira V Beier in November 1981.

- The first AKC UDX was Lee Catlett's Cammcastle's Abel Warlock UDX.

HCH/WTCH Rojan's Ground Zero, Am/Can HX, ATD s/d/c, H-RD IIIs, HTDIIs, HTDI. (B. Davenport)

Langrave Salem von Brabant, UDTX was the first Rottweiler to earn the novice Agility title. He is also a Junior Herding Dog. (John Quay)

- The first AKC UD TDX was William Salathiel's Ebonstern Ladonna VD Liebe, UDTX, in April 1982.

- The first AKC herding–titled Rottweiler was Barbara Davenport's Paragon's Maserati, *Herding Started* (HS) title, in the fall of 1994.

- The first AKC herding excellent title in June 1996 and the first AKC herding champion in June 1997 was Rojan's Ground Zero owned by Barbara Davenport and Janet Mester.

- The first AKC Novice Agility–title was earned by Tricia and Wayne Millsap's Langrave Salem Von Brabant, UDTX in October 1994.

- The first AKC Open Agility–titled Rottweiler was Marlita Dougherty's Zebediah Von Strobel, UD in October 1994.

CH West Winds Ayla, UDX, B, HIT, HC, CGC, RTD, doing what she loves to do. (Roger LeMar)

- The first AKC Agility Excellent was awarded to Barbara Budnar's U-CDX, U-AgI Abigale Vom Haus Gordon, CDX, in March 1997.

- The first AKC Variable Surface Tracker and Champion Tracker was CT Rodsden's J Socrates v Quira, CDX, owned and trained by Jack Hlustik, in April 1996.

Since the two of us are also into the working aspects of this versatile breed, we would like to honor the AKC Obedience Trial Champions as true Rottweiler headliners. As a result of the dogs' innate character and the owner/trainers' dedication, these dogs have done more for the good name of Rottweilers in the general public's eyes than any Best in Show winner. These are the dogs the public sees doing things for their owners and behaving in a polite and civilized manner. The Best in Show winner, on the other hand, is seen only as a pretty dog, with no thought about his temperament.

Rottweilers That Have Achieved the AKC Obedience Trial Championship (OTCH)

1. OTCH Mondberg's Donnamira V Beier
   Bitch bred by Mrs. S. Parker
   Owned and trained by G. Beck

2. OTCH Way-Mar's Disco Dawg
   Bitch bred by L. Leoni
   Owned by W. and M. Sohlman

3. OTCH Dolly Vom Odenwald, TD, SchH I
   Bitch bred by W. and V. Absher
   Owned and trained by Ann Aummers Schuch

4. OTCH Magnum Von Meadow III, TDX
   Dog bred by D. Wormser
   Owned and trained by E. Swancer

5. OTCH Way-Mar's Rocky Racoon
   Dog bred by W. and M. Sohlman
   Owned and trained by B. Kiefer

6. OTCH Carla Vom Kasseler Hof
   Bitch bred by I. Freguia
   Owned and trained by E. Verkozen

7. OTCH Masty Sunde Vom Tanzenfeld
   Bitch bred by D. and A. Johnson
   Owned by V. and L. Sunde

8. OTCH Summer's Glory Da Bratiana
   Bitch bred by M. Law
   Owned and trained by A. Summers

9. OTCH Rock Solid Risky Business, UDX
   Bitch bred by W. Harris
   Owned and trained by B. Kiefer

10. OTCH Elsa S Geer, UDX
    Bitch bred by B. Burke
    Owned by C. and J. Geer

11. OTCH Rennick's Bedazzled On Sunde, UDX, TDX
    Bitch bred by Pat Riley
    Owned by V. and L. Sunde

Rather than go on and on about individual dogs, we would like to honor the longtime breeders who have made those great show dogs possible. The following list is of those American breeders who have been at this long enough to have produced five generations of their own stock. We apologize if we have missed anyone; it was pure oversight and certainly unintentional.

Breeder	Kennel Name
Bill Alexander	Lowenhart
Jonathan Bratt	Bratiana
Sue Catlin	Der Catlin
Rebecca Chriscoe	Von Ursa
Evelyn and Jack Ellman	Von Stolzenfels
Debbie Gallegos	Lauffeuer
Judy Hassed	Von Arktos
Judy Johnson	Graudstark
Jane Justice	Windrock
Jeff and Gerry Kittner	vh Kertzenlicht
Felice Luburich	Srigo
Shelly Moore	Merrymoore
Klem and Rademacher	Rodsden
Joan Reifman	Haserway
Margot Schmidt	Vom Odenwald

Some Rottweilers are so talented they can skateboard! This is Panzer von Siegerhaus. (T. & C. Woodward)

Breeder	Kennel Name
Catherine M. Thompson	Von Gailingen
Thelma Wade	De Riemer
Shirley Werner	Wernerhafen
Cheryl Wheeler	Ebonstern
Tom and Carol Woodward	Von Siegerhaus

(Thompson)

CHAPTER 12

What You Should Know About Breeding

You have a Rottweiler and probably paid what you consider a lot of money for him. You think, "I can raise Rottweilers as an income generator." There are many important considerations before deciding to breed your dog. This chapter will give you insight to enable you to make a sound decision on whether or not to breed your Rottweiler.

The first consideration should be whether or not your Rottweiler is purebred. Do you have AKC papers for your Rottweiler? Is your Rottweiler's individual AKC registration nonrestricted? Breeders do not check the Limited Registration box by mistake. If your Rottweiler's AKC registration is limited, he should not be bred, and if bred, any offspring of his cannot be AKC registered. If your Rottweiler is not purebred or does not have a full AKC registration, he should be neutered.

Where you got your Rottweiler is the next consideration. Did you get him from a pet store, an animal shelter or did you find him? If he was obtained from any source other than a reputable breeder, you cannot know enough about the background of your Rottweiler to know what genetic problems he may have. Without knowledge of potential genetic defects, you will run the risk of bringing puppies into this world who will go through much pain and suffering and can cause the new owners pain and suffering because they require a lot of medical treatment or must be euthanized.

EVALUATING YOUR ROTTWEILER

If your Rottweiler was obtained from a reputable breeder, did you get a five-generation pedigree for your dog? Are there at least four titled dogs (Champion, Obedience, Tracking, Herding, Agility, Schutzhund) in the first three generations? If not, why not? Were they not sound enough in body to compete? Were they not sound enough in temperament to compete? A breeder who says "I just want to sell pets, I don't care about showing or training dogs" does not care enough about the Rottweiler. A good breeder should be concerned

Does the Rottweiler you plan to breed have any working ability?

about preserving the characteristics that make a Rottweiler a Rottweiler. Generations of Rottweilers who have not been allowed to work will lose the traits that distinguish them from any other breed.

In your five-generation pedigree, are there health certifications such as Orthopedic Foundation for Animals (OFA) and Canine Eye Registry Foundation (CERF)? If not, why not? What do you know about the health of the dogs in your Rottweiler's pedigree? Do you know what characteristics should be avoided when choosing a mate for your dog?

How is your dog's temperament? Has he passed AKC's Canine Good Citizenship test? If he hasn't, why not? Do you really know the difference between aloofness or shyness and aggression?

Before you even contemplate breeding, evaluate your stock. This is CH Rodsden's Heika v Forstwald, CD, VB, TT, an ARC Gold Dam. (Michels)

Does your Rottweiler have any disqualifications or serious faults according to the AKC standard for Rottweilers? (See Chapter 3, "Official Standard of the Breed with Interpretation," for a full review of the official standard.) Is your Rottweiler considered a good specimen of the breed? Please remember that there are no "rare" Rottweilers. Dogs that are red, blue, green-eyed or any other variation of the standard are probably not purebred Rottweilers.

Is your Rottweiler sound, healthy and certified free of genetic diseases? If not, why? Not living near a veterinary specialist or not being able to afford the examinations and certifications is not a good excuse.

EVALUATING YOURSELF

Are you a good record keeper? If not, you must learn to be if you want to breed AKC-registered

Careful selection of complementary parents produces promising offspring like this 8-month-old bitch.

dogs. This applies to the owner of both male and female dogs. AKC does spot check your records and will suspend your privileges to register dogs if you are not compliant. The AKC states that

> *All required records must be made immediately when the dog is acquired and delivered, and at the time of mating, whelping or death. Records must be kept on forms devoted to that exclusive purpose and must be consecutive, accurate, up-to-date and maintained for at least five (5) years after the dog has died, has been sold or has been given away.*

Furthermore, these written records, if kept on computer, must also be kept on a separate printed copy (hard copy) and not just on disk.

The AKC requires detailed records be kept of all breedings and their outcomes.

RECORDS THAT MUST BE KEPT

- The breed
- Registered name and number
- Sex, color and markings
- Date of birth
- Names and registration numbers of sire and dam
- Name of breeder
- Name and address of person from whom directly acquired
- Date of acquisition
- Date and duration of lease, if dog or bitch is leased from another person
- Name and address of person to whom directly sold or delivered
- Date sold or delivered, or date of death
- Types of papers and date supplied
- Dates and place of mating
- Names of persons handling the mating
- Registered name and number of dog to which mated
- Name and address of owner of dog to which mated
- Date of whelping
- Number of puppies whelped by sex and by color and markings
- Litter registration number
- Date of sale, gift or death of each puppy
- Name and address of person acquiring each puppy
- Registered name and number of each puppy registered by breeder

The AKC requirements can make IRS record-keeping requirements pale in comparison, so be prepared before you consider breeding your Rottweiler.

Last, but not least, if you own or house more than one dog of the same breed, you must also have a system such as marking, tagging or tattooing each dog for identification. Contact the AKC for a copy of the rules and regulations for registration and identification of dogs.

No carefully bred Rottweilers go unidentified. (Piusz)

WHY BREED?

Let's assume that your Rottweiler is of breeding quality. Why do you want to breed him? Are you actively training or showing him and truly want to improve the breed? If your reasons for breeding your Rottweiler are to make money, to let your children see something being born, because you think he should be bred before neutering or because you think it will calm him down, please do not breed your Rottweiler. Our breed deserves more than that.

Jane Justice's Windrock Rottweilers are bred with purpose.

Consider Time and Expenses

Now assume that you have a sound, healthy, titled Rottweiler that fits the standard and has a true Rottweiler temperament and you are anxious to breed him. Are you prepared to take the time and handle the expense of breeding? Just how much time and expense varies, but here are a few anecdotes to give you an idea.

A Rottweiler breeder in Canada calls her puppy Jib because the cost of whelping and raising the litter took the money they had saved to purchase a sailboat. Breeders have named puppies Budget Buster, Brinks and Last Dollar to describe the cost of whelping and raising litters. If there is a lawsuit involving a dog bite by a purebred dog, the breeders and owner of the sire are usually named in the suit. One owner of a Rottweiler stud dog was sued for the value of a dog and future litters,

It can cost a lot of money to whelp and raise even a small litter.

because the bitch being bred to his dog escaped and was killed by a car. Breeders have used vacations and leaves of absence from work to hand-raise litters when the dam died shortly after birth.

Hundreds of other examples come to mind, and as experienced breeders often say, "My veterinarian will soon expand his office and name a new wing after me because I've spent so much money there."

The discussions of breeding in this chapter relate to Rottweilers. There are many very good "how-to" books available that you should read before deciding to breed your Rottweiler. We offer the following information to enlighten you so that you can be prepared for the true costs and liabilities of breeding Rottweilers.

Reponsible breeders keep track of their puppies throughout their lives, good or bad. (K. Yontz)

A Real Responsibility

Neither the owner of the sire nor the owner of the dam is released from the ethical and potentially legal responsibilities of bringing Rottweiler puppies into the world until each of those puppies is no longer alive. If you either knowingly or ignorantly are responsible for Rottweiler puppies who carry serious hereditary health or temperament problems, and those puppies grow up and are bred,

you are never ethically released from the responsibility of serious harm to the Rottweiler breed. You could be the cause of heartbroken families and Rottweilers in pain for many years to come.

Rottweiler owners must also constantly evaluate whether a dog or bitch should be bred again. The ideal of Rottweiler type, conformation and temperament might not be a good producer. Evaluate not only the puppies, but the breeding/whelping/mothering process. A dog who will never instinctively breed a bitch on his own, a bitch who will never stand for a dog, a bitch who cannot whelp

Mothers are the best teachers. Pups learn about life and how to react to it from their dams.

puppies without a C-section, a bitch who is a terrible mother and a bitch who has eclampsia with every litter should not be bred. Although human interference can cause these problems occasionally, repeated incidents are a message from nature that breeding is not for this Rottweiler.

IF YOU THINK YOU'RE READY

What is the single most important consideration in breeding Rottweilers? It is finding a good mentor and becoming a student of the Rottweiler. You must study everything you can about the Rottweiler and about dogs, including genetics, health issues and canine behavior. You must join your local Rottweiler club, the American Rottweiler Club and your local kennel club. Ideally, your mentor will be the breeder of your dog and can advise you on the strengths and weaknesses in your dog's pedigree. You can never learn enough.

One last statement regarding the decision to breed or not to breed: The Rottweiler is a working dog, and any person who breeds Rottweilers must be prepared to advise puppy owners on training, behavior and show matters. If you have not trained a Rottweiler to an Advanced Working or Obedience title *and* put an AKC championship on a Rottweiler, you are not experienced enough to be a responsible breeder. There is no substitute for hands-on experience.

THE MALE

Most people assume that there is little work or worry for a stud dog owner. Simply put, this is a wrong assumption.

Having a mentor will make breeding more educational and rewarding for you. This is Cathy Thompson. (G. Shagauwat)

Your male Rottweiler will need some tests done at the veterinarian before he can be used at stud.

Before you offer your Rottweiler "at stud," he must pay a visit to his veterinarian for a few tests. The most important test is a *brucellosis* test. Brucellosis is a venereal disease that can be transmitted to humans. If your male Rottweiler is not *proven* (that is, has not fathered live puppies), he should have a sperm count and motility test.

Your Rottweiler or his veterinarian might not be thrilled with the sperm-collection part of this test, but a bitch owner deserves to know that the stud dog is not sterile. Sperm collection in Rottweilers is accomplished the same way it is with men (but without the visual aids). The veterinarian who must do the manual stimulation of your Rottweiler probably will not do it without your presence because your dog will be more relaxed and able to perform better with you there. If you want to own a stud dog, you must be prepared to stand in an examination room with a veterinary technician and your veterinarian while your Rottweiler is being manually stimulated to ejaculate.

Sound unpleasant and embarrassing? It's nothing compared to what you might have to do during a breeding, so if you can't cope with a semen collection, you really shouldn't breed your male Rottweiler.

The stud dog should be current on his vaccinations and heartworm testing and should be free of internal and external parasites. No bitch owner wants to treat a pregnant bitch for fleas, ear mites or worms, especially if she got them from the stud dog. Except for the sperm count and motility test, all the tests and checks for parasites and current

A/C CH Bluewater Zeus Von Zolty, CD, is ready for the girls. (Goodwin and Glynn)

vaccinations mentioned previously must be done every time your stud dog is bred.

Now that you have determined that your male Rottweiler has a high sperm count with good motility, is free of diseases and parasites and is otherwise in great shape, you must put together his "resume" so that the bitch owner can determine that he is the right dog for the job.

Put together information packs on your prospective Romeo that include a five-generation pedigree; a copy of his AKC registration certificate; copies of his OFA, CERF, heart or other health certifications; copies of his title certificates and photographs of Romeo himself. Making color laser copies is a good way to copy photographs for this project. The information pack must also include Romeo's stud contract, which is described in more detail in the next section. These packs should be given to each bitch owner who displays an interest in your stud dog.

THE STUD CONTRACT

Why do you need a stud contract? What should be included? Ethically and for your protection, you should provide a stud contract for your dog. Because money, or a puppy who has a value, will change hands as a result of a mating, both parties should have a clear agreement of the expected

outcome and further actions if the outcome of the mating is not live puppies. Matters like these are always best put in writing before the breeding so that there are no misunderstandings.

The AKC takes the position that the owner of the sire of a litter is required to sign the application for registering a litter to certify that the particular dam was bred to the sire on a specified date, unless there is an agreement signed by all concerned parties that the sire's owner will not sign the application until the stud fee is paid. If there is no written agreement, you could be required to sign the form, the dam's owner could register and sell puppies and you could still be trying to collect your stud fee.

The stud contract should include, as a minimum, the following information for both the male and female:

Include a photo of your stud dog in his stud packet you send to prospective bitch owners. This is CH Windrock's Hotstuf v Richter.

Will these two make a suitable pair? Only the breeders can determine that.

- Names.

- Registration numbers.

- Titles.

- Health certification numbers (for example, OFA and CERF).

- Dates of mating.

- Due date of the litter for each breeding.

- Terms and mode of payment of the stud fee.

- What constitutes a litter (for example, one live puppy surviving to six weeks, or two live puppies at birth)?

- When the stud dog owner will be paid (for example, half of the stud fee at the time of mating and the remainder when puppies are born, or the pick of the litter at eight weeks).

- What happens if the bitch fails to conceive? (Does she get a return service, and is it only at her next heat? What happens if your stud dog is no longer available?)

Last, but not least, get the stud contract signed before you let your dog breed any bitch.

If a bitch owner has looked at your stud dog, studied your dog's resume and wants to breed his

Your dog may not have much to say about his potential mate, but you should.

bitch to your Romeo, you should request from the bitch owner the same information that you supplied. You should also see the bitch and evaluate her temperament and conformation. Will she complement your dog? Do they have the same faults? Look in her mouth, check her bite and count her teeth. The time of breeding is too late to discover that she has a disqualifying bite or missing teeth.

Approve the Bitch

If you are uncomfortable asking questions about a bitch, looking at her bite and otherwise checking her over, remember the first rule of dog breeding: The stud dog always gets the blame for any fault, disease or other anomaly in a litter of puppies. Even though both parents contribute equally to the genes of the puppies, the father always gets the blame. If you love your male Rottweiler so much that you can't bear to have anyone criticize him or say "He throws this or that," do not breed him.

Likewise, if you want to continue having nice bitches come to your stud dog, be sure of what he is being bred to. One bitch with a serious problem that she has passed on to the puppies can give your dog the reputation for causing that problem, even if it's not true.

If you love your male so much you may not be able to tolerate possible criticisms of his progeny, don't breed him.

The bitch owner should supply a copy of AKC registration, health certifications and proof of negative brucellosis and fecal tests. The bitch should appear in good condition and be free of external parasites.

All the arrangements with the bitch owner should be made well before the bitch comes in season. A bitch owner who calls and says that he would like to breed to your dog and that his bitch has just come into season usually doesn't plan the raising of a litter properly. Your dog and his offspring deserve a better start than with a breeder who can't take time to plan a proper mating for his bitch.

BRING IN THE BITCH

Finally, you have done everything you should and Romeo's big day has come. What should you expect? It is customary for the bitch to come to the male. This means that the stud dog owner must be prepared to keep the bitch at least three to four days at no charge to the bitch owner if she will not be brought by the owner for each attempted breeding. Either way, your day-to-day routine will be very different for up to two weeks.

If the bitch is sent in, you are responsible for her care. You might have to pick her up at the airport and arrange to have her flown back. If you are very lucky, she is crate trained, will not mind a stranger going into her crate to put a leash and collar on her to take her out to potty, will not try to escape from your fence or dog run, will urinate or defecate on lead if you don't trust her loose in your fenced yard (from experience, this is a good idea), will go willingly back into her crate, will eat and drink with no problems, will not whine or bark and will not chew up her crate pad. The bitch's owner will always assure you that his "girl" will be the perfect angel. Rottweiler bitches in season usually surprise their owners—owners are always saying, "I can't believe she wouldn't go back in her crate for you," or "She whined all night? She never does that at home."

There are other interesting aspects of boarding a bitch in heat, especially if you usually do not have a nonspayed bitch living with you. She will spot your floor from the time she gets out of the crate until she goes out the door. And she probably will spot on the way back, too. There is an odor

Your bitch may have to leave home to be bred. Discuss all these details in advance of the breeding.

to estrus, especially in a large breed like the Rottweiler, and it is detectable to the human nose, especially in the room occupied by the bitch's crate.

Expect the Unexpected

While the bitch is at your house, and for some time after she is gone, your Romeo will become a Rottweiler that you might not particularly like. He will do most of the following, if he is at all a typical male: refuse to eat; scent mark your house with urine (especially a corner near the room where the bitch is housed); mount you, your children, the cat, and other dogs—even other males; become a dog fighter; challenge you or your family; open doors you never thought he could; jump through the window; chew his way into the room with the

bitch and whine, bark, hoot and howl longer and louder than you ever thought possible. Regardless of the size or layout of your house, you will not be able to get your dog far enough from your bedroom to get a good night's sleep. You might hear of ways to stop the unpleasant behavior, such as putting vanilla or Vicks VapoRub on Romeo's nose. Although we can only speak for Rottweilers and Linda's Smooth Fox Terrier male, this does not work.

"Super" Romeo

If you think you will avoid the unpleasant male behavior by insisting that he only be bred to bitches whose owners bring them for the mating and do not leave them with you, you might be surprised. Not only can Romeo

Your male will be very excited to have a bitch in season at his house and may behave in unexpected ways.

exhibit the aforementioned traits, but you might also find that he can jump your fence with a single bound and disappear looking for Juliet.

Whether the bitch is brought in by the owner or is in your care, you might think that the obnoxious behavior of your Rottweiler will cease as soon as the mating has occurred. It usually doesn't and usually escalates after the dog and bitch are introduced for the actual mating because your timing, the bitch owner's timing, the bitch's veterinarian's timing and the two dogs' timing are never the same. Most Rottweilers will not breed until they are ready. Eager first-time Romeos might try to breed a bitch who is not yet receptive by mounting her head, side or even the correct end, but the not-ready Rottweiler bitch might try to render Romeo incapable of ever breeding anything.

What does this timing discussion mean to you as the stud dog owner? Your schedule has just been changed, Romeo has had a close encounter with a bitch in season and now *really* has reason to howl at night, you have to keep the bitch longer than you expected and your lifestyle is interrupted longer than you planned. If the bitch is brought by the owners for each breeding, you have to deal with them more times than you expected, you begin to wonder if Romeo will get the job done and you realize that you might have gone through a lot of trouble—there might be no breeding—for no stud fee at all.

THE MATING

Because it is customary in Rottweilers for there to be two breedings (ties), the "try the breeding/

they're not ready" routine could go on for a week or more. As a Rottweiler male becomes more experienced, there will be more "she's not ready" episodes because he will know when he's ready and will perform on his schedule only.

Regardless of what your Romeo says, the bitch's owner has gone to great effort and expense to use your dog and is entitled to that service. Therefore stud owners must be prepared to achieve that end, whether that means helping Romeo hit the target, building him a stool for those tall girls or going to the vet's office at their own expense for a semen collection and artificial insemination.

We know that it sounds funny talking about a stool for the stud dog, but sometimes it is necessary. Almost anything can and probably has been

The process of breeding your Rottweilers is more complicated than you'd expect, but the results can be worth it.

used, including digging a hole for the bitch. Just remember that the dog's hind feet are going to be beside the bitches, so if she's in a hole, so is he. What Cathy uses for a stud stool are two six-foot-long two-by-tens spaced about ten inches apart. The bitch is simply walked in between them, and Romeo is now nearly two inches taller.

Timing

If you try to trick Mother Nature with artificial insemination techniques because you do not want to keep the bitch, you will probably find that you have spent time and money for nothing. Nature doesn't like to be hurried, and the bitch will probably not get pregnant. And, of course, there's the embarrassing trip to the veterinarian with Romeo and Juliet, where, besides the awkwardness of the collection of Romeo's semen, some veterinarians might ask you to keep an eighty pound–plus Rottweiler bitch's rear end elevated for up to fifteen minutes with a gloved finger in her vagina to stimulate the contractions of a natural breeding (while someone else holds Romeo for fifteen to forty-five minutes until he loses his erection and is able to walk again).

One last word of advice on timing: If the bitch's owner says the vet did a smear and she's definitely ready, it might not mean much unless the bitch owner has taken the bitch for every day of estrus, the smear has been fully cornified for four days, the bitch has not been stressed by shipping or other factors and the bitch has a documented history of vaginal cytology/successful breedings for several previous heats. You probably understand the "timing is unpredictable" point by now. Think we're exaggerating? Talk to a Rottweiler stud dog owner or your Rottweiler's breeder; you'll probably hear a story about a bitch who wouldn't conceive until her twentieth day of heat and another about a bitch who was always bred on her seventh day. We can say "Been there, done that."

Place and Preparation

Assuming that it finally is the right time and you still want a stud dog, what do you do? You do not turn the two Rottweilers loose in the back yard together. You must find a place for the mating with good footing for the dogs and lots of cushioning for your knees that is out of public view and that you don't mind getting dog slobber and other fluids on. It also has to be a large enough area that at least two human adults and two adult Rottweilers can easily maneuver in it and be comfortable for up to an hour.

Some preparation is required before the tryst. If you are unable to stay on your knees comfortably for up to an hour, you should place a milk crate or short stool in the area to sit on for up to an hour. Don't bother placing books or magazines to read in the area—you won't be able to do that while you wait. A telephone in the area is a good idea, too, with your veterinarian's phone number close by (if you have been so lucky in dogs that you haven't memorized it yet). Last, but not least, place towels and paper towels within reach. Invest in a good, comfortable basket muzzle that will fit an adult Rottweiler bitch and have it handy.

The dogs may be game to breed anywhere, but you need to control the time and environment to prevent mishaps.

Holding the Bitch

Once the area is prepared, it's showtime. Bring the bitch into the area first. She should be on leash and wearing a good collar. Now you, as the stud dog owner, must make a big decision—to muzzle or not muzzle the bitch. If the bitch's owner will witness the mating, hopefully, you have already discussed this point. We have a simple rule about muzzling a Rottweiler bitch if she is being bred to our stud dogs: If we have not bred that same bitch previously and do not know from personal experience whether she will misbehave, we muzzle her. Why? Because we are protective of our stud dogs and ourselves. We hold the bitch, even if the bitch's owner is present if the owner is not experienced

with breeding Rottweilers. *Holding* means being down on your knees, with a firm grip on the bitch's collar with one hand and the other hand supporting her under her belly so that she can't sit down. With experience, you'll learn which way your stud dog turns, so you will know which side of the bitch is easier to support.

A first-time bitch owner may declare "rape" at this point. To the true anthropomorphic, any forcing of another to have sexual intercourse is rape; however, by that definition, all dog breeding is rape, since the dogs do not get to choose their mates. You are simply ensuring the safety of your dog and yourself. Since the stud dog has not been brought into the area yet, the bitch owner has the option to leave with no breeding if he can't stand to see his baby muzzled and supported during her encounter. Do not give in, do not remove the muzzle and do not decide against holding and supporting the bitch. A Rottweiler bitch, especially if not ready to stand, can be very unpredictable when a male tries to enter her. She can whirl around and bite you in the face. She can turn in a second and give your dog a nasty bite to the penis. She can suddenly sit down or try to run away when the dog has entered her.

It's Not All Romance

With the bitch muzzled and securely supported, your stud dog should be brought into the mating area on leash. He should have a flat collar on that will enable someone to grab it easily to pull him off in case of a "false start." Bring Romeo up to the bitch before taking him off lead. Many

Rottweiler males will act goofy and will mount the bitch's head. Pull him off immediately if he's not mounting the proper end. Romeo only has one chance for the day, and if he is allowed to become fully erect, he cannot enter the bitch and the opportunity to breed is lost.

Rottweiler males will usually lick the bitch's ears, back and neck, as well as her vulva, which can be rather unpleasant for the holder of the bitch. If the bitch is ready to be bred, she will lift her vulva to accept the male and *flag* by moving her tail to one side. When Romeo finally mounts and begins to thrust, he might need to be guided into the vulva. This is usually accomplished by cupping a hand just under the bitch's vulva and guiding the penis in. Yes, it's messy, but if you don't do this, Rottweiler males are so large that you might not see the penis become trapped between the bitch's back and the dog, which will provide stimulation for the ejaculation and thus cause the breeding opportunity to be lost.

When a Rottweiler dog has entered a bitch, he'll thrust very hard while gripping the bitch's back with his front legs and doing a little dance with his rear feet. The person holding the bitch will get slobbered on and might get scratched. The dog might also grip so hard that he pinches the arm supporting the bitch's belly. If the person holding the bitch lets go and the bitch moves, the breeding opportunity could be lost. Hold on tight and be prepared for the Rottweiler bitch to cry out loudly at this time.

When the dog has stopped thrusting, he'll probably start the turn himself. However, some Rottweiler males seem content to just stay there on the bitch's back. This is hard on the bitch and the person holding her, so help him turn. Rear-end to rear-end seems to be the most comfortable position for Rottweilers during the tie. And during the tie is when the person holding the bitch really starts to develop an aching back.

Breaking the Tie

When the tie breaks, Rottweilers can leave behind a lot of fluid, so be prepared. Both the dog and bitch will lick themselves. Take the dog away from the bitch to an area where he can rest and have access to water. Watch him closely during this time because male Rottweilers can have the skin at the tip of the prepuce roll inward while the penis is moving back into the sheath. He will cry out, and you must pull the sheath back to ensure that the penis withdraws entirely into the sheath and is not left exposed to dry out or become injured.

If you have read this far, you can see how involved owning a Rottweiler stud dog can be. Unless your Rottweiler male is truly outstanding, he shouldn't be bred. And even if he is outstanding, you still must be prepared to manage him properly. You also must be strong enough in character to tell the owner of an unworthy bitch that your dog will not be bred to her. You owe it to the Rottweiler breed to be selective.

We have reached an era of scientific progress, and the freezing and storage of sperm is now readily available to stud owners. If your dog proves to be an outstanding producer, the time for collecting and freezing the semen is when the dog is in his prime, which is between four and six years of age. Doing it sooner means that you have gone to some expense and effort that might not be necessary, and doing it later might mean poor collections and lower sperm quality. Be sure that the sperm bank is an AKC-approved facility.

THE BITCH

If you own a Rottweiler bitch and want to breed her, read the male section carefully. She too, will need a "resume" prepared to send to stud dog owners that includes a five-generation pedigree; a copy of her AKC registration certificate; copies of her OFA, CERF, heart and other health certifications; copies of her title certificates and photographs. She should be free of external and internal parasites and in excellent health. She must also take a trip to the veterinarian for a brucellosis test and proper vaccinations. A urinalysis, blood chemistry and thyroid screen are strongly suggested for Rottweiler bitches. This small investment in tests can save the Rottweiler bitch owner thousands of dollars in stud fees and expenses by detecting a problem that can cause failure to conceive.

A bitch owner must study pedigrees and spend time looking at male Rottweilers and their offspring. A top show winner is not necessarily a good producer, so careful observation of a dog's offspring is important in determining whether he is a good producer. You must find a dog who will complement your bitch, and without research and the advice of a good mentor, you won't be able to do that.

Living with Her Highness

What is it like to live with a nonspayed Rottweiler bitch? "Usually messy," is what you're likely to hear. Rottweiler bitches in heat are capable of spotting a lot and making your house a mess, and many have a very strong odor associated with estrus. Many Rottweiler bitches experience changes in disposition with the hormonal changes associated with estrus, such as becoming bossy toward other dogs. While your bitch is in heat, she is banned from obedience competition, she might be banned from training classes, she must be kept confined, your children might be mounted by male dogs, wandering male dogs might try to get

Eleven-year-old CH Michael's Leea can include CD and CGC Certificates on her "resume."

into your yard, your own male will act as described earlier in this chapter, she might mark your house and she might try to escape to meet males. It is very common for Rottweiler bitches to come into season every four months rather than every six months. Like owning a stud dog, your lifestyle will change when your Rottweiler bitch is in heat.

If you feel that you must breed your bitch, you must be prepared to take the time and make the investment of properly raising and placing Rottweiler puppies. You must be willing to take the risks associated with breeding—the chance of losing your bitch, needing a C-section for your bitch, losing puppies and dealing with sick puppies. This all can (and probably will) happen if you breed long enough.

Not for the Money

It is very expensive to breed a Rottweiler bitch and raise a litter of Rottweiler puppies. Often, it is more expensive than the money received from the sale of puppies. Over time, it always costs more than the money received from selling puppies. You cannot make money on puppies if you do it right. If you don't want to do it right and think you'll make money, you could find yourself in a lawsuit because you sold a puppy who was unhealthy or unsound in temperament.

There are many outstanding books on the breeding of dogs, and Rottweilers whelp in the same way as all other dogs. They are as unpredictable as any breed regarding the date to breed and whelp. Since there are so many good books that describe whelping and the care of puppies,

Potential brood bitches should have strong, correct heads.

we will not go into great detail on this topic as we did on the topic of mating, which is seldom described. Before your bitch is bred, you must read as many of these books as possible. We've included a list in the bibliography.

BITCHES AND PUPPIES

There are some things we consider noteworthy when raising Rottweiler puppies. Good mothers tend to produce good mothers, and poor mothers tend to produce poor mothers. If your bitch is not a good mother, she should not be bred again.

Many books mention eclampsia, a calcium metabolic disorder, as a problem with bitches of smaller breeds. Rottweiler bitches can develop it, too, and it is life-threatening. To avoid eclampsia and other problems, take care not to oversupplement during a Rottweiler bitch's pregnancy. Many times Rottweiler bitches go into a preeclamptic state while in the process of whelping. We recommend giving a calcium supplement during whelping to prevent this condition. Signs of preeclampsia are growling at the newborns or pushing them away when they try to nurse. Simply giving a couple of extra-strength Tums after the third or fourth whelp will prevent the condition. Continue to give the bitch Tums for two to three days, morning and evening, and that should do the trick.

Proper socialization of Rottweiler puppies is a must. This takes time with a litter but has to be done. There can be no compromise during puppy raising, so think about your available time from the due date and at least the eight weeks following the birth when you are planning to breed. The novelty

of a new litter wears off fast when the work and time involved become a reality, so be prepared for that, too. Rottweiler puppies make an amazing mess, and it's not limited to cleaning the potty section of a puppy box. Rottweiler puppies wear more food than they eat, and each puppy must be cleaned after feeding, which will happen four times a day. Socialization time is above this normal maintenance requirement, so plan, plan, plan.

Puppies and their mother can also be the cause for concern when things don't go as planned, and they rarely ever do. Tail docking, eclampsia, mastitis, infection, not enough milk and dehydration are just a few of the very common worries a breeder faces with each litter. Placing Rottweiler puppies in the right homes is another worry. Many breeders will not breed a bitch who will have a litter that will be ready to go to new homes between Thanksgiving and Christmas because puppy buyers during the holiday season will not take the time a Rottweiler puppy needs to develop into a wonderful adult.

Rottweiler puppy buyers need counseling from puppyhood to old age. You must be prepared to tell owners how to deal with housebreaking, chewing, play biting, training, showing, a veterinarian who is uncomfortable with Rottweilers, neighbors who are afraid of their dog and, especially, male adolescence. If you have never owned a male, how will you accomplish this?

RISKS AND REWARDS

Breeding Rottweilers is a lifetime responsibility consuming lots of time and money. It involves costly visits to veterinary specialists, can result in

This mom puts up with her energetic youngster.

Your puppy buyers should feel free to call and ask you about their dog's behavior anytime.

heartbreak and will disrupt lifestyles. It is not a get-rich-quick scheme. Yes, it can be rewarding, which is why some of us do it, but it is a long process that requires the highest ethical and moral standards and a clear vision of what you want to accomplish. It cannot be done properly without learning from a good mentor and lots of research. Our Rottweilers deserve responsible owners, and breeding for the wrong reasons is simply not responsible. You can never go wrong by spaying or neutering your Rottweiler.

After reading this chapter, you might wonder why anyone would breed Rottweilers. We can tell you that we are both very proud of owning American Rottweiler Club Gold Production Award Dams. We enjoy training and living with different generations of our breeding. Neither of us has produced the perfect Rottweiler, but we can still try. The greatest reward, however, is the satisfied owner of a Rottweiler from our breeding program. A thank you and a story about how wonderful a Von Gailingen or Lindenwood pet Rottweiler is makes it all worthwhile. After all, all of our puppies are pets first, then some are shown.

(Justice)

CHAPTER 13

Special Care for the Older Rottweiler

There is nothing more wonderful than an old Rottweiler. Most breeders will tell you that ten years is the average lifetime for a Rottweiler. Fortunately, with better-quality dog foods and more awareness of health issues, there are many twelve-, thirteen- and fourteen-year-old Rottweilers alive today.

Old Rottweilers know so much. They will potty, eat and drink on command. They know what "no" means. If you open the door, they understand "wait." They have house manners. They let you get a good night's sleep. They don't chew. They are mellow. They know the routine. They know what is expected of them. They are confident in themselves and don't challenge for their position in the pack.

THE AGING PROCESS

Most Rottweiler specialty shows that offer veteran classes specify the minimum age for a veteran as seven years old. The average Rottweiler hits his prime at four to five years old. He is generally well-bodied then and mature mentally. Generally, gray hairs start to show on the muzzle around age six, and muscle tone becomes harder to maintain at age seven. However, some bloodlines have very little gray and are still athletic at age eleven.

Like most dogs, Rottweilers can develop arthritis as they get older. Rottweilers are large-boned and substantial, and it is very common that they will develop arthritis in their toes. If your Rottweiler has hip dysplasia or another orthopedic problem, arthritis will develop in other joints, too. Your veterinarian can prescribe a *nonsteroidal anti-inflammatory drug* (NSAID) to relieve the symptoms, or you can explore other options of treatment with your veterinarian.

SIGNS OF OLD AGE

Rottweilers will begin to lose muscle tone and coordination as they get older. Because of this, slippery floors are a problem for older Rottweilers. Walking across a bare wood, linoleum or tile floor will become difficult, as will getting up from a bare

Chula, CDX, (sitting) is 11 and helping her friend Rosco celebrate his 12th birthday

floor. Cover the floor with a nonskid-backed rug to help your old dog's mobility.

Arthritis and loss of muscle tone in old Rottweilers make them very sensitive to pressure on their bony areas, such as elbows and hips. They appreciate egg-crate pads, either homemade or purchased orthopedic types. You can purchase egg-crate foam from a discount department store, cut it to size and cover it with blankets or synthetic sheepskin to make a comfortable bed. Rottweilers like to be with the family, so put several "beds" around the house for your old dog's comfort.

Old Rottweilers can experience hearing and sight loss. Be aware of this, especially if you think that your old dog is constantly ignoring you. Although there is little you can do about it since it is part of the aging process, you can assist your dog by touching him to get his attention before asking him to do something. If your old dog is outside and off leash, remember that you must be responsible for his whereabouts, and don't let him wander off. If you lose him, he might not be able to hear you call him, and he can easily get himself in a very dangerous situation.

Senior Rottweilers are more sensitive to hot and cold temperatures than younger dogs. They can become easily overheated in hot weather. If the humidity is high, an older dog is especially susceptible to heatstroke or heat exertion. They are also more sensitive to the cold and can become very sore and stiff if they have been shivering. Be very aware of your old Rottweiler's comfort in warm or cold weather.

Weight gain is common in old Rottweilers, who become less active. Excess weight can

Older Rottweilers are more sensitive to temperature—hot and cold.

aggravate existing problems and lead to new ones, like diabetes, so it is important to keep an old Rottweiler at a good weight.

Old Rottweilers stress easily and generally prefer a routine in their daily lives. They want to be fed and walked on the same schedule every day and like to sleep at the same times. If you must change his routine or make a radical change, like rearranging furniture or moving to a new house, be very sensitive to your dog's needs. Give him lots of attention and support to help him adjust to the change.

While old Rottweilers do like routine, they also enjoy doing things they did when they were younger. For example, a camping trip, boat ride or car trip can make an old Rottweiler very excited. But the older dogs can overdo it, so remember that moderation is necessary and watch for signs of stress. Older Rottweilers will need more frequent stops than they did when they were younger. Also, remember to take along a well-cushioned mattress or pad for your dog to rest on.

NUTRITION

Diet plays an important role in weight control. Exercise is important, too, and your older Rottweiler should continue to exercise as much as he is able.

Your older Rottweiler probably doesn't need a change of diet just because he's a senior. The diet he's been getting as an adult should be fine, as long as he's healthy and not gaining weight. However, as your Rottweiler gets older, he will appreciate several smaller meals per day rather than one large meal per day. When you begin to introduce several

They may be older, but these Rottweilers still enjoy an active, outdoorsy life.

meals, remember that the quantity of food per day should stay the same. If your Rottweiler is eating three cups of food once per day, he should receive three one-cup meals in a day. One cup of food doesn't look like enough, but remember that two more meals are coming and your dog will be happier without the extra pounds.

If you notice a weight gain, decrease the amount of food you are feeding, as long as your dog's hunger is abated. If you don't feel that your Rottweiler will be receiving adequate nutrition from a reduced amount of food, ask your veterinarian to recommend a senior or "light" dog food, which will make your dog feel full with fewer calories.

Many older Rottweilers will have a gradual loss of appetite. Senses of smell and taste can decrease in older dogs, which makes food less appealing. Your older Rottweiler's teeth and gums can affect his appetite as well. If he seems to be avoiding his crunchy kibble, have your veterinarian check his mouth for problems. To increase the appeal of your Rottweiler's food, you can try warming it, but take care that it is not too hot. Some older Rottweilers like soupy food, so add unsalted beef or chicken broth. Other older Rottweilers simply prefer a change in brand of kibble. With older Rottweilers, be sure to make any change in diet gradually.

If your Rottweiler experiences a sudden loss of appetite, or his appetite has diminished to a dangerously low level, consult your veterinarian. This could signal a serious illness. If your dog does experience a serious loss of appetite, you might have to cook for him and feed him by hand. This will not spoil him, and when he feels better, he will begin eating on his own again.

It is very tempting to give your old Rottweiler a few more treats than usual. If you give him treats, be sure that they are wholesome and not too fatty or salt-, sugar- and additive-laden. Changes from his normal diet can cause gastrointestinal upset, especially if he consumes too many treats like pigs' ears.

Generally, it is not necessary to give your older dog supplements if he has a nutritionally sound diet. Many Rottweiler breeders suggest vitamin C supplements, among others, but be aware that vitamin C causes diarrhea if the dose is too high and is not introduced gradually. It is always a good idea to consult your veterinarian about supplements, and it is important that you tell your veterinarian if you are giving supplements to your Rottweiler. Your veterinarian cannot give your Rottweiler the

As your Rottweiler gets older, continue to feed him an optimal diet, and resist the urge to give him too many snacks. (Lee Whittier)

best treatment if he doesn't know what supplements your dog is receiving.

Your senior Rottweiler must have a constant supply of fresh water. Older Rottweilers might have trouble getting up and down or moving around, and they sometimes simply forget to drink and do not go to their water bowl often. Observe your older dog's drinking habits to be sure that he does not get dehydrated. Even mild dehydration can be serious for an older Rottweiler.

Most people place their dog's food and water bowls on the floor. It can be uncomfortable for an older Rottweiler to bend down to eat and drink, though, so it is advisable to raise his bowls off the floor. Many food and water stands are available at pet supply stores and through catalogs, but a round wastepaper basket or a piece of ten-inch diameter PVC pipe will hold some stainless steel bowls perfectly too.

To keep your older dog interested in his water, thoroughly wash and refill his water dish several times per day. Consider setting out water bowls in several locations that he can reach easily. If he hasn't had a drink in a long time, take the water bowl to him. Most older Rottweilers will respond to a command such as "Get a drink."

Your senior Rottweiler will want to be included in his regular routines of eating, exercise and playing and everything else you do.

EXERCISE

Older Rottweilers need exercise for their well-being. They need it to maintain proper weight, to benefit normal body processes and to combat boredom. However, older Rottweilers do not have the stamina of younger Rottweilers, so you must adjust the duration of the exercise to your older dog's needs.

If your senior Rottweiler has not had a thorough checkup by his veterinarian and has not been exercising regularly, get the checkup before starting an exercise program. Even with a veterinarian's OK, observe your dog carefully during and after exercise sessions for signs that he is overdoing it. Coughing, difficulty in breathing, lameness and a drooping head are signs that the exercise is too much. It is also prudent to have your veterinarian examine your Rottweiler if he exhibits any of these signs during exercise.

Your aging Rottweiler also has aging joints. Walking on leash is wonderful exercise, but remember, two shorter walks are preferable to one long walk. Intensive exercise like running is not recommended for an older Rottweiler, since arthritic changes and diminished muscle tone can cause stress and injury to joints and soft tissue.

If your senior Rottweiler likes to swim, let him. However, he can become chilled easily, so take several large towels with you and dry him off thoroughly as soon as he gets out of the water.

Most Rottweilers like to play fetch or chase a Frisbee, and this still applies to older Rottweilers. Throw the ball, stick or Frisbee a short distance for the old dogs, and only a few times. Old Rottweilers will still enjoy the game and feel proud that they have played ball, even though the ball was only thrown ten feet. Be very careful with a game of fetch and an old Rottweiler who is not so steady on his feet—he can fall and injure himself easily. You might need to improvise and play a game of fetch with a favorite toy on a carpeted

If your dog is the Frisbee-catching kind, continue to play the game with him, just taper it slightly.

area indoors. A gentle tug-of-war with an old Rottweiler can also be fun.

Old Rottweilers might not realize that they can't do what they once did and might become overexerted. Limit and closely supervise their exercise. Arthritis is common in older Rottweilers, and without a warm-up and cool-down period before and after more strenuous exercise, your old dog can develop very painful inflammation. Heavy dogs such as Rottweilers can develop sore feet, so check your Rottweiler's feet for cuts and abrasions before and after every walk.

GROOMING

Grooming is an excellent way to monitor your older Rottweiler's health. Brush him at least once a week, taking care to check for new or changing lumps or wounds, parasites or unusual discharges. Check his ears, pads and mouth during this weekly session. Check between his toes for cuts or lumps. Trim his nails. Long nails will cause sore feet and mobility problems.

Short nails, clean teeth, clean ears and manual/visual checks for lumps or sores will make your old Rottweiler feel good and give you early warning of any potential health threats. It will also keep doggy odor and bad breath at bay, which will make him more pleasant to be around.

If you used a grooming table when your Rottweiler was younger, you might want to switch to grooming him on the floor when he gets old. Lifting an old Rottweiler onto a grooming table can be painful for him, and he will probably be happier lying on his side on the floor while you

A reunion of Roma Rottweilers still looking good. (Martin)

won't be around much longer. This is good and bad for the old dog.

When you bring a new pet into the family, it is most important to remember that the old Rottweiler has been part of the family for a long time and needs to understand that he is still important. It is easy to devote lots of attention to the newcomer and take the old dog for granted. Give the old dog special attention to make him feel that he is still important.

Old Rottweilers need their rest. Give the old dog breaks from the new arrival and ensure that his sleep and rest routines stay normal.

Old Rottweilers can become very protective of "their things." What *you*

groom him. Sitting on the floor beside your dog, you can brush, trim nails and do all the other grooming with little stress on your old dog. If he still protests nail trimming, teeth cleaning or ear cleaning, put him on leash and tie him to a doorknob or other object. This is similar to a grooming noose and stabilizes him while you work. Don't think that your old Rottweiler will be less stressed if you forget about grooming because he doesn't like it. He will be far more stressed if a pending health problem goes unnoticed and develops into a serious condition.

INTRODUCING ANOTHER PET

When your Rottweiler gets old, you might decide to get a puppy or other pet because you figure he

A new puppy may reinvigorate your old dog, or it may depress him.

consider an old dog's possessions and what *he* considers his might be different. The water bowl, for example, can become the object of an altercation. Monitor all encounters between newcomer and old-timer closely for the first few weeks to protect both parties from an unpleasant dispute.

On the other hand, a new playmate can make an old Rottweiler feel young again. Monitor play sessions, and don't let the old dog play too long or too hard.

WHEN THE TIME COMES

Unfortunately, old Rottweilers do not live forever, and sometimes tough decisions must be made for them. We all hope that our old dogs will die quietly in their sleep or while doing something they really enjoy. Sadly, it doesn't always happen like that. Rottweilers deserve their dignity at any age,

Four generations of Rottweilers. Junior gives grandma a kiss. (G. & R. Martin)

and there might come a time when euthanasia is the right choice for them.

The pride, aloofness and independence that cause us to love the breed are the same characteristics that help us decide if it is time for euthanasia. If Rottweilers cannot exhibit these characteristics, they are not happy and their quality of life is very poor. If pain, inability to get up on his own, inability (or refusal) to eat or drink on his own or other infirmities strike your old Rottweiler, please listen to what his eyes and actions are telling you. You will know that it is time for euthanasia.

What do you do when it is time to euthanize your old Rottweiler? The answer is simple: You help him through it. This old friend deserves your company to the end. He would sacrifice his life to protect you and would never abandon you, so now you must not abandon him. If you feel that you just can't do it and would rather have someone else take him to the vet to put him down, then get counseling before the time comes. Consult your veterinarian, the Internet or a local funeral home for preeuthanasia counseling (it does exist) or grief counseling to help you deal with the loss later. If you cannot get over it and help your friend during euthanasia, then you don't deserve to own a Rottweiler or any dog for that matter. Rottweilers deserve unselfish owners, especially at the end of their lives.

Now that we've established that you will be there for your old dog, should you take him to the veterinarian or ask your veterinarian to come to your home? A lot depends on your relationship with your veterinarian, but many veterinarians will

You owe it to your old friend to listen to what her eyes and actions tell you about how she's feeling.

make house calls for euthanasia. It might depend on your Rottweiler's opinion of a trip to the veterinarian. Most Rottweilers love to go to the vet, but some are stressed by it. If you take your dog to the veterinarian's office, you can also request that your Rottweiler be euthanized in the car.

Once it has been established where the euthanasia will take place, the veterinarian will usually have a veterinary technician help him with the procedure. Most of the time, your Rottweiler will be asked to lie down. You should position yourself so that your dog knows you are there, so that you can pet and comfort him during the process and so that you are not in the veterinarian's and veterinary technician's way. If your Rottweiler is on the floor or in your car, you can sit with the dog's head on your lap. If he is on the table, you can hold his head and comfort him.

How Euthanasia Works

What happens during euthanasia? Basically, your dog is given an injection of a drug, usually a highly concentrated barbiturate, that reduces central nervous system activity. This depresses all the functions controlled by the brain stem, causing a loss of consciousness and cessation of the heart function. There is also depression of the respiratory function, but the other effects are more rapid. As far as can be determined, unconsciousness precedes heart failure, and the process is painless.

While the veterinarian is preparing the injection, talk to your Rottweiler. Tell him what a good friend he has been, pet him, tell him you'll miss him and cry if you want. Veterinarians have pets, too, and understand that this is a great loss to you and your family. This is the time to comfort your dog, not to worry about appearances.

The veterinarian will usually place a tourniquet on your dog's leg to find a vein for the injection. The veterinarian will try to make this as easy on your dog as possible. He might seek a location other than the front leg if it will be too hard on your dog to get the front leg vein.

As the drug enters your Rottweiler's system, he will become unconscious and his breathing will change. The process can take several minutes before your old friend takes his last breath, but remember, he is not in pain. He might appear to gasp for breath, but again, it is a reaction to the effects of the drug, and he is not aware of what is happening. If your dog's bladder is full, he might urinate as his muscles relax just before and after death. Keep this in mind if your dog is being euthanized at home or in your car, so that you can place something under your dog to protect carpeting or upholstery. A minute or so after your dog's last breath, the veterinarian will listen for heart sounds to confirm the death. When the death is confirmed, you can ask to be left alone with your dog for a few minutes, if you desire.

There are many ways to prepare your old Rottweiler for euthanasia, when the time comes. If your Rottweiler is old and it is clear that euthanasia might be necessary soon, some veterinarians can prescribe Valium (for the dog—not you) to give your dog before you put him in the car for the ride to the vet's. For a very old Rottweiler in poor health, this might depress him just enough that he will die before you get to the vet's office. If he isn't refusing food entirely, some owners pick up a milk shake or ice cream on the way to the vet's office so their old companion can go while eating something he really likes. The whole family might want to spend a few minutes with their old friend; then the children can leave the room just before the euthanasia. You know your old dog, and you can determine what is best for him at this time.

With an old Rottweiler, it is prudent to decide what you will do with his remains after death. If you plan to bury him, remember, he is a large dog requiring a very large hole in the ground. You should check local ordinances which may prohibit burying your dog in your yard. If it is the middle of winter, you will not be able to dig a suitable hole in frozen ground. Your veterinarian can usually suggest a service that will keep your Rottweiler's remains frozen until the ground thaws or recommend a crematorium. Your vet can dispose of your dog's remains if you do not want burial or cremation. Although it is an unpleasant task to think about what to do with your dog's remains before his demise, planning ahead makes the task easier when the time comes.

(Courtesy of the American Rottweiler Club)

CHAPTER 14

The American Rottweiler Club

There are many clubs around the country for Rottweiler fanciers. Membership in these clubs is a way to meet other Rottweiler owners and breeders and to learn more about the breed. Most of these clubs are either American Kennel Club sanctioned or are German-style clubs. Both types are well worth joining for the camaraderie of fellow Rottweiler owners and the educational programs they offer.

If the clubs are *American Kennel Club* (AKC) sanctioned, they are known as *local clubs* or clubs that are restricted to a particular locale. The AKC also sanctions one club on a national level; that club is referred to as the *parent club*. The *American Rottweiler Club* (ARC) was founded in 1973. The AKC has sanctioned the ARC as the parent club for Rottweilers in the USA.

Being the parent club means that the ARC and its members have control of the breed standard for Rottweilers in America. The parent club, ARC, is also the only club allowed to be a member of the American Kennel Club, a club of clubs. With ARC's membership in the AKC comes the ability to send a delegate to the AKC meetings, where rules, regulations and policies on registration, shows and events are established. In other words, the American Rottweiler Club is the only club that has a say about Rottweilers with the American Kennel Club.

Membership in the ARC brings like-minded Rottweiler enthusiasts together.

The National Specialty offers all AKC events in which Rottweilers are eligible to compete. At the 1998 nationals, there were two Agility trials, two Obedience trials, a Herding test and trial, a Tracking and Tracking Dog Excellent trial, a Top Twenty competition (the top twenty show dogs from the previous year compete under three judges), sweepstakes for puppies and veterans (an informal conformation competition for puppies and dogs older than seven years of age) and, of course, a Conformation show. The event takes almost a week to accomplish.

Attending the National Specialty gives Rottweiler fanciers plenty to watch and opportunities to meet new friends,

Membership in the ARC is particularly important for breeders and dog show exhibitors. Because of the ARC's member status and its delegate, it has a vote on matters of importance to Rottweilers.

ARC SPECIALTY SHOWS

The ARC does more than just send a delegate to the AKC. It offers specialty shows—dog shows limited to Rottweilers only. The ARC sponsors up to eight regional specialties per year and one national specialty. The ARC's National Specialty rotates around the country so that all Rottweiler fanciers have the opportunity to attend.

The ARC national specialty attracts the top dogs in the country, including Gold Sires like A/C CH Von Gailingen's Matinee Idol, UD, TDX, Can CDX, HIC, CGC, UX. (Thompson)

The ARC supports the accomplishments of Rottweilers in all endeavors. (Thompson)

visit with old friends, see the top dogs in the country and attend several educational seminars. It is well worth the time and effort to attend.

Other ARC Offerings

The ARC also sponsors many educational programs. It has a breeder referral service. If you call the AKC and have questions about Rottweilers, you are forwarded to the ARC's Breeder Referral Committee. This committee refers you to a breeder in your area of the country. The ARC also has a puppy booklet and an illustrated breed standard available to the public at a nominal charge. An ARC flyer with this information is included with all AKC Rottweiler registrations.

ARC Web Site

The ARC also has a wonderful Web site that is chock-full of information. You can access it on the Internet by going to www.amrottclub.org. There you'll find answers to frequently asked questions, the illustrated standard, a schedule of ARC shows, training tips and health issues and a list of local Rottweiler clubs.

As a service to our wonderful Rottweilers, the ARC offers production awards to any Rottweiler who qualifies. This award is to recognize outstanding producers. See Appendix D, "The Hall of Fame American Rottweiler Club Production Awards," for more details.

The ARC also awards medallions to the top ten Rottweilers in AKC events. They give these medallions to the dogs, whether or not the owner is a member; ARC is one of the very few clubs to do so. Top Ten medallions go the ten best show dogs; show bitches; junior handlers; Novice, Open and Utility Obedience Rottweilers; Herding and Agility Rottweilers. The ARC also offers a special plaque to all Rottweilers who qualify as Obedience Trial Champions, Champion Trackers, Herding Champions and Master Agility Dogs.

NOT JUST SHOW DOGS

You might think that the ARC is only interested in show dogs. This is untrue. The ARC has established a series of awards that recognizes our

This Rottweiler even loves agility in the rain. (Pet Portraits)

most versatile dogs. The Versatility awards are given to those Rottweilers that prove themselves to be truly versatile in terms of performance events.

These are for the dogs, so the owners do not even have to be ARC members. Check out the ARC Web page for all the details (www.amrottclub.org).

Epilogue

We hope that this book has given you an appreciation for the Rottweiler and his unique character. While Linda and Cathy would not change breeds for the world, that does not mean the Rottweiler is for everyone. His strong will, independent nature and desire to make decisions require an equally willful and determined owner.

If you were to compare the Rottweiler to the equine family, the Rottweiler would be a mule, while the German Shepherd Dog would be a horse. More people can get along with horses and make them perform as desired than they can with mules. The mule is generally smarter, more sure-footed, stronger and has more endurance than the horse. The person who gets the desired performance from a mule is a special type. Once a person has had a positive experience with mules, he is very likely to stick with them; it is the same with Rottweilers.

Some of us feel that the Rottweiler can leap tall buildings in a single bound and catch bullets in his teeth—a superdog! However, this is not the general public's opinion of our beloved breed. Rottweilers are thought of as killer dogs—vicious black menaces that should be banned from cities and towns.

It is every Rottweiler owner's responsibility to ensure that the public's view of the Rottweiler is changed. That opinion must be changed to one of accepting these large, black and tan dogs as just that: large, black and tan dogs. This responsibility includes proper socialization, training and control of your dog. Rottweilers must only be seen as well-mannered, polite canine citizens entitled to a place in any civilized society. Whether the Rottweiler earns the respect of the general public is up to you, his owner.

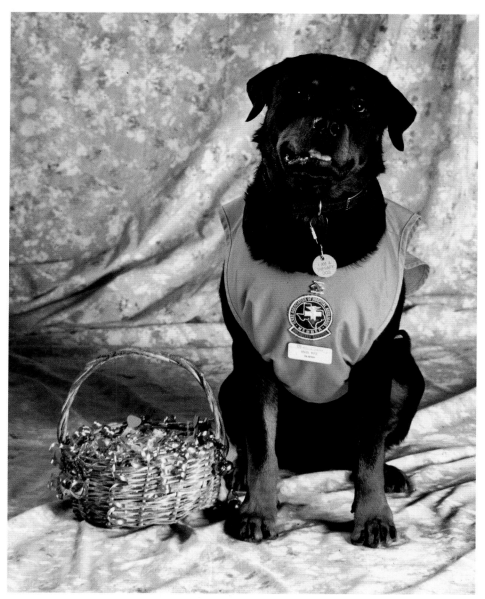

(Donna and Karl Rice)

Organizations and Other Resources

American Herding Breed Association
1548 Victoria Way
Pacifica, CA 94044
www.primenet.com/~joell/ahba/main.htm

American Kennel Club
Customer Service
5580 Centerview Dr.
Raleigh, NC 27606-3390
(919) 233-9767
or
Administration
51 Madison Avenue
New York, NY 10010
(212) 696-8200
www.akc.org/

AKC Gazette and *The AKC Events Calendar*
Diane Vasey, Editor
American Kennel Club
51 Madison Avenue
New York, NY 10010
Subscriptions: (919) 233-9767
www.akc.org/gazet.htm
www.akc.org/event.htm

American Rottweiler Club
9840 S. Hamburg Road
Whitmore Lake, MI 48189
www.amrottclub.org/index.htm

**American Temperament
Test Society, Inc. (ATTS)**
P.O. Box 397
Fenton, MO 63026
(314) 225-5346

**Australian Shepherd Club of America
(ASCA)**
Business Office
6091 E. State Highway 21
Bryan, TX 77803-9652
(409) 778-1082 (business office)
(209) 539-5802 (Education)
www.asca.org/

Canine Eye Registration Foundation (CERF)
Veterinary Medical Database/Canine Eye
Registration Foundation (VMDB/CERF)
Department of Veterinary Clinical Science
School of Veterinary Medicine
Purdue University
West Lafayette, IN 47907
(317) 494-8179
www.vet.purdue.edu/~yshen/cerf.html

Direct Book Service
701 B Poplar
P.O. Box 2778
Wenatchee, WA 98807-2778
(800) 776-2665
www.dogandcatbooks.com

Dog Fancy
(article reprints/back issues)
P.O. Box 6050
Mission Viejo, CA 92690
(714) 855-8822
www.dogfancy.com/

Dog Lovers Bookshop
New York, NY
www.dogbooks.com

Dog World
(article reprints/back issues)
500 N. Dearborn, Suite 110
Chicago, IL 60610
(312) 396-0600
www.dogworldmag.com/subscribe/

Friskies Canine Frisbee Disc Championships
4060 D Peachtree Road, Suite 326G
Atlanta, GA 30319
(800) 786-9240

Front and Finish
(obedience monthly newspaper)
H & S Publications
P.O. Box 333
Galesburg, IL 61402-0033
(309) 344-1333

International Weight Pull Association (IWPA)
P.O. Box 994
Greeley, CO 80632
www.eskimo.com/~samoyed/iwpa/index.html

Landesverband DVG America (Schutzhund)
113 Vickie Drive
Del City, OK 73115
http://webusers.anet-stl.com/~dvgamer/

National Association for Search and Rescue (NASAR)
4500 Southgate Place, Suite 100
Chantilly, VA 20151-1714
(703) 222-6277
www.nasar.org/

National Dog Registry
(tattoo registry/lost and found)
P.O. Box 116
Woodstock, NY 12498
(800) NDR-DOGS
www.natldogregistry.com/

North American Dog Agility Council, Inc. (NADAC)
HCR 2, Box 277
St Maries, ID 83861
www.teleport.com/~jhaglund/nadachom.htm

North American Flyball Association (NAFA)
1400 W. Devon Ave.
Box 512
Chicago, IL 60660
(309) 688-9840
http://muskie.fishnet.com/~flyball/

Orthopedic Foundation for Animals (OFA)
2300 E. Nifong Blvd.
Columbia, MO 65201-3856
(573) 442-0418
www.offa.org

Therapy Dogs International
6 Hilltop Road
Mendham, NJ 07945

United Kennel Club
100 E. Kilgore Road
Kalamazoo, MI 49001-5598
(616) 343-9020
www.ukcdogs.com/

United Schutzhund Clubs of America
3704 Lemoy Ferry Road
St Louis, MO 63125

U.S. Dog Agility Association (USDAA)
P.O. Box 850955
Richardson, TX 75085-0955
(214) 231-9700

You can find a list of local Rottweiler Clubs on the American Rottweiler Club's Web page at www.amrottclub.org

(Isabelle Francais)

The American Rottweiler Club Mandatory Practices

(Reprinted with permission from the ARC)

These Mandatory Practices are established in accordance with the objectives of The AMERICAN Rottweiler CWB. Adherence to these MANDATORY PRACTICES is required of all members. Introduction: The Rottweiler is above all a working dog and must exhibit the temperament, intelligence and structure of a working companion. The physical appearance should be as described in the Rottweiler Standard approved by the American Kennel Club May 8, 1990.

AS AN ARC MEMBER, I SHALL ADHERE TO THE FOLLOWING MANDATORY PRACTICES:

1. Study and strive to conserve and improve the breed in structure, temperament and working ability, never sacrificing one for the others.

2. Breed only AKC registered dogs and bitches which have OFA certified hips (or HD-free hips as certified by foreign counterparts of the OFA). Imported Rottweilers must have OFA hip certification within six months after arrival in USA. If frozen semen is used from an imported Rottweiler,

the dog must be x-rayed and certified by the OFA or foreign counterpart at no less than 24 months of age. Breed only dogs and bitches of stable temperament with no disqualifying physical faults according to the ARC Rottweiler Standard (i.e., entropion, ectropion, overshot, undershot, wry mouth, two or more missing teeth, unilateral cryptorchid or cryptorchid males, long coat, any base color other than black, absence of all markings).

3. Offer at stud with a signed, written contract only mature (two years of age or older) healthy dogs with OFA certified normal hips, free of communicable diseases, having none of the faults listed in Section 2 above. Refuse stud service to any bitch not meeting the same requirements.

4. Breed only bitches two years of age or older with OFA certified normal hips, in good health, free of communicable diseases, having none of the faults listed above in Section 2, to not more than one stud dog at any one season, and not more than two out of three consecutive seasons. Plan all litters with the goal of improving the breed.

5. Maintain the highest possible standards of health, cleanliness and care of all dogs. Dogs shall be contained within safe restrictions when the breeder/owner cannot personally supervise their safety.

6. Choose names for ARC registration which do not use prefixes or kennel names associated with other recognized breeders of Rottweilers in the U.S., Canada, Germany or any other foreign country, unless written permission is obtained from the original user of the name.

7. Sell all dogs with a signed written contract. All dogs/puppies sold must be guaranteed to be in healthy condition, including adequate protection against known diseases. Keep and pass on to buyers accurate health, breeding and registration records and pedigree records of at least three generations. Registration papers may be withheld or breeder's rights retained only by mutual agreement in writing, signed by both parties. Require that all Rottweilers not purchased as show and breeding stock be made incapable of reproducing, and require that limited registration blue slips be provided, or that registration papers be withheld until a veterinarian's certificate is received as proof of sterilization. Release puppies to their new home only after they reach seven weeks of age.

8. Evaluate honestly according to the ARC Rottweiler Standard. And state clearly to the Buyer the quality of any Rottweiler sold. All advertising shall be honest and informative and shall in no way misrepresent the stock offered. Prices shall be based on individual merit and shall not be included in any advertising.

9. Sell only to responsible persons and do not knowingly sell to anyone or any entity who engages in any activity which might exploit the breed. Rottweilers shall not be given as prizes, offered in raffles or sold at auctions,

nor shall Rottweilers be exploited in any detrimental manner.

10. Breeders recognize that they have a lifetime responsibility for puppies produced by their breed bitch or stud dog. Breeders and stud dog owners recognize the inherent obligation to provide a stable environment that protects each puppy's physical and emotional well-being. This includes helping to relocate to a new home a puppy (or adult dog) with which the owner is dissatisfied, or taking that puppy (or adult) back. Any provisions for refunds or reimbursement of expenses shall be handled in the contract between breeder and owner. No puppy or adult dog bred or owned by an ARC member shall be disposed of in an animal shelter or pound unless required to do so by law.

11. Observe the highest standards of sportsmanship and good will at shows, obedience and herding trials, and at any other event involving Rottweilers. Assist all newcomers to the breed so that they may be guided in the ways that can best conserve and improve the Rottweiler.

AS AN ARC MEMBER, I SHALL ENCOURAGE THE FOLLOWING RECOMMENDED PRACTICES:

1. Encourage working titles to retain the breed's correct working temperament. Encourage the showing of future breeding animals in the conformation ring, keeping in mind that the purpose of such shows is to improve the breed by objective evaluation of the animals in competition according to the Breed Standard.

2. Encourage the recommendation that all dogs should be tattooed or microchipped in an individual and identifiable manner before having hips x-rayed. Also encourage the recommendation that all dogs have their eyes checked yearly by a veterinary ophthalmologist and that the presence of other hereditary diseases such as elbow dysplasia, von Willebrand's disease, subaortic stenosis and hypothyroidism be checked for prior to breeding.

As a member of the American Rottweiler Club, I have read and understand that I shall be required to abide by the above Mandatory Practices in all ways. I understand that these Mandatory Practices are applicable to all dogs owned, co-owned or leased by or from me. I further agree to abide by the above Recommended Practices to the best of my ability.

I understand and agree that upon receipt of sufficient written proof of violations of these Mandatory Practices, the Board of Directors will proceed according to the Constitution of the American Rottweiler Club, Article VI. A Grievance Committee of five members is to be appointed by the Board of Directors as required to report their findings to the Board for a vote by the Board. I further understand and agree that should I, through no fault of my own, be in violation of any of the aforementioned provisions, I shall have recourse to the Grievance Committee appointed by the Board of Directors.

The Meaning of All Those Titles

A guide to abbreviations of titles and words often found in Rottweiler pedigrees

AMERICAN KENNEL CLUB (AKC) ABBREVIATIONS

AJX	Agility Jumpers with Weaves Excellent	Third level of jumpers with Weaves Agility program.
AX	Agility Excellent	Third level of Agility.
BIS	Best in Show	Best dog at an all-breed show.
BISS	Best in Specialty Show	Best Rottweiler at a show where only Rottweilers compete.
BOB	Best of Breed	Best Rottweiler at an all-breed show.

BOS	Best of Opposite Sex to Best of Breed	After Best of Breed (BOB) is awarded, the best that is the opposite sex of that BOB.
BOW	Best of Winners	The best between the Winners Dog (WD) and the Winners Bitch (WB).
CD	Companion Dog	Primary Obedience degree earned from the Novice class in Obedience. Akin to a high school diploma.
CDX	Companion Dog Excellent	Secondary Obedience degree from the Open class in Obedience. Akin to a college diploma.
CGC	Canine Good Citizen	Very simple test of a dog's deportment, manners and temperament.
CH	Champion	Won fifteen points (including at least 2 major wins) under three different judges. Relating to beauty, conformation (structure and movement), showmanship and breed type. Different requirements for different countries.
CT	Champion Tracker	A dog who has earned Tracking Degree (TD), Tracking Degree Excellent (TDX) and Variable Surface Tracker (VST) titles.
Gr I-IV	Group 1 through Group 4	Awarded to dogs who place First through Fourth in the Working group at an all-breed event.
HCH	Herding Champion	Title earned after completing the Herding Excellent title, earning 15 championship points in the Advanced classes with at least 2 first place wins.
HE	Herding Excellent	Titled earned after 3 qualifying legs in the Advanced Herding class.
HI	Herding Intermediate	Second level of Herding titles, earned after 3 qualifying scores in the intermediate classes.
HIC	Herding Instinct Certificate	Certificate earned after passing 2 herding instinct tests.
HITs(dg)	Herding Instinct Tested in sheep (ducks or goats)	Basic test of herding instinct in sheep, ducks or goats.
HS	Herding Started	First level at Herding trials.

HT	Herding Tested	First pass/fail test; must be passed twice to earn title.
Leg		Like the "leg" of a journey, dogs competing for a Companion Dog (CD), Companion Dog Excellent (CDX) or Utility Dog (UD) Obedience title are required to earn three legs toward each title.
MA	Master Agility	Title earned after the Agility Excellent (AX), with 10 qualifying runs at the Excellent level.
MAJ	Master Agility Jumpers with Weaves	The forth level of the Jumpers with Weaves Agility program.
Major		Refers to three-, four- or five-point shows. Computed by AKC geographically and statistically.
MX	Master Agility Excellent	Title earned after earning an Agility Excellent title and qualifying at 10 trials in the Agility Excellent class.
MXJ	Master Excellent Jumpers with Weaves	Highest level of the Jumpers program, akin to a championship.
NA	Novice Agility	First of the Agility titles.
NAJ	Novice Agility Jumpers with Weaves	First level of Agility Jumpers with Weaves division.
OA	Open Agility	Second level of Agility title.
OAJ	Open Agility Jumpers with Weaves	Second level of the Jumpers with Weaves Agility program.
OTCH	Obedience Trial Champion	Highest level of Obedience achieved. Akin to a doctorate—and then some!
Points		Zero to 5 points (of 15 required) are awarded to Winners Dog (WD) or Winners Bitch (WB) at AKC-licensed events.
PT	Pretrial Tested	Second test level in Herding.
RTD	Registered Therapy Dog Certified	Certification by a national therapy dog organization that dog has met criteria.
RWD/RWB	Reserve Winners Dog/ Reserve Winners Bitch	The "second best" dog or bitch in the classes on a given day.

Select		Awarded *only* at the American Rottweiler Club's National Specialty to the judge's final few selected for consideration for Best of Breed. Often misused.
TD	Tracking Degree	Test of a dog's scenting and tracking ability.
TDX	Tracking Degree Excellent	Advanced Tracking Ability test.
Top Ten		Usually refers to the top ten Rottweilers competing in the nation during an annual time period. Can refer to Top Ten Obedience, Top Ten Working Group or All-Breed Dogs.
TT	Temperament Test certified	Certificate awarded after passing an American Temperament Test Society Test.
UD	Utility Dog	Third Obedience degree from the Utility class. Akin to a master's degree.
UDX	Utility Dog Excellent	A dog has qualified in both the Open and Utility class on the same day at 10 shows.
UDT	Utility Dog Tracker	A dog has earned both Utility and Tracking Dog titles.
VST	Variable Surface Tracker	A Tracking title earned on a track that is 70 percent without vegetation.
WD/WB	Winners Dog and Winners Bitch	Winner of the male and female champion points, respectively.

FOREIGN ABBREVIATIONS AND TERMS

AD	Endurance Dog title	Endurance run of 20 kilometers.
ADRK	Allgemeiner Deutscher Rottweiler Klub e.V.	The *only* German club recognized by the American Kennel Club (AKC), Verband Für das Deutsche Hundewesen (VDH) and Fédération Cynologique Internationale (FCI). Maintains the Stud Book for Rottweilers only.
BBT	Basic Breed Test	Same as the ZtP, minus the protection work.

BH	Begleithund or Traffic Sure Companion Dog title	Includes on- and off-leash Obedience and Temperament test.
BST	Breeding Suitability Test	Same as the ZtP/Ztpr.
FCI	Federation Cynologique International	The official International Canine Federation—a show-giving organization, not a registering body.
FH	Fährtenhund	Advanced Tracking exam.
Gekört		Qualified to breed for a term of two years.
Gekört bis EzA		Qualified to breed for breeding lifetime of dog (dogs from 2 to 9 years; bitches from 2 to 8 years).
HD-	HD-Frei	Indicates that the dog is free of hip dysplasia.
HD+/-		Indicates slight changes to hip joints.
HD+		Indicates that mild hip dysplasia is present; dog is not eligible to take ZtP, effective 1/96.
HD++		Indicates that hip dysplasia is present; dog is never eligible for breeding.
HD+++		Indicates severe hip dysplasia; dog is never eligible for breeding.
INT CH	International Championship	*Only* awarded by the FCI in accordance with its rules.
IPO		International Working Test title.
Körung		Advanced Breeding test. Incorporates working, conformation and producing ability.
SchH	Schutzhund	Three-phased German dog sport and breed test, including tracking, obedience and protection. There are 3 levels: I, II and III.
SG	Sehr Gut	Rated Very Good.
Sieger		Best male in a German Rottweiler show. BS is the title for best male at the Bundes show (or German National dog show), and KS is the title for best male at the ADRK's Klub show.

Siegerin		Best female in a German Rottweiler show. Bsg is the title for best female at the German National Show, the Bundes show.
V	Vorzüglich	Rated Excellent.
WH		Watchdog title.
ZtP	Zuchttauglichkeitsprüfung	Breeding Suitability test that incorporates hip rating, conformation and basic working ability. Also abbreviated Ztpr.

HEALTH ABBREVIATIONS AND TERMS FOUND IN PEDIGREES

CERF	Canine Eye Registration Foundation	Canine ophthalmologists test and certify eyes against genetic diseases annually.
OFA	Orthopedic Foundation for Animals	Canine radiologists rate and certify x-rays of hips and elbows after the age of 24 months. This is a basic requirement prior to mating. E = Excellent, G = Good, F = Fair.
Thyroid-		Indicates that the thyroid gland's hormonal levels have been tested and found to be within normal limits; translates to thyroid-negative or thyroid-free.
VWD-	von Willebrand's disease–free	A genetic bleeding disorder.

The Hall of Fame: American Rottweiler Club Production Awards

These awards are open to all Rottweilers, living or dead, who have distinguished themselves by their American-titled offspring. As production points accumulate, the individual sire or dam may receive the next higher award.

To be eligible for any award, a Rottweiler must have done the following four things:

- Produced at least one AKC Champion of Record

- Produced at least one Advanced Working–titled dog (CDX, TDX, VST, SchH I, HI or OA)

- Produced at least three titled offspring

- Met the production point requirements

	BRONZE PRODUCTION AWARD	SILVER PRODUCTION AWARD	GOLD PRODUCTION AWARD
Males	25 points	50 points	75 points
Females	15 points	30 points	45 points

Production points are calculated as shown here:

BREED	OBEDIENCE		TRACKING		SCHUTZHUND		HERDING		AGILITY	
CH 3	CD	1	TD	1	BH	1	HT	1	NA	1
	CDX	2	TDX or VST	5	SchH I	3	PT	1	OA	2
	UD	3	CT	3	SchH II	2	HS	2	AX	3
	UDX	3			SchH III	2	HI	3	MA	3
	OTCH	3			FH	4	HX	3	MX	3
							HCH	3		

Working titles are cumulative. For example, a CD is one point and a CDX is two points, for a total of three production points (CD plus CDX).

You must apply for these awards. The application must contain the name of the dog or bitch, breeder, owner, owner's address and phone number. It must also contain the names and titles of the offspring. In order to verify the titles, the application must contain either the issue of the *AKC Awards* magazine in which the title was published or a photocopy of the title certificate. Schutzhund titles must be verified by a photocopy of the scorebook or the page in *USA* or *DVG* magazine in which the score is published. The owner does not have to be a member of the American Rottweiler Club.

If you are having problems with the verifications, contact Cathy Thompson.

Send applications to:

Cathy Thompson
1579 Rock Bridge Rd. SE
Washington Court House, OH 43160-9721

American Rottweiler Club Production Awards as of April 1998

NAME	TITLED OFFSPRING	POINTS
Gold Sires (75 or more points)		
Amboss Vom Konigssiek, SchH III, FH, IPO III	9 CH; 4CDX; 22 CD; 1TD; 2 NA; 28 BH; 2 SHI1; 1 SH2; 2 SH3	117
CH Amos Von Siegerhaus	17 CH; 7 CDX; 23 CD; 2 TD; 1 PT	98
CH Barto VT Straotje, TD, IPO III	10 CH; 2 UD; 3 CDX; 11 CD; 1 TD; 2 BH; 1 SH1; 1 SH2; 1 SH3	80
Select CH Birch Hill's Governor, CD	39 CH; 2 UD; 5 CDX; 25 CD; 2 TD	171
CH Birch Hill's Minuteman, CD	24 CH; 4 CDX; 22 CD; 1 TDX; 2 TD	114
CH Birch Hill's Quincy, CD, TD	23 CH; 3 UD; 7 CDX; 18 CD; 8 TDX; 1 PT; 2 BH; 1 SH1	189
Select CH Boss of Hale's Hollow, CD	23 CH; 1 CDX; 9 CD; 1 NA	82
Brando Vom Dattelner HOF, SchH II, FH	25 CH; 1 CDX; 7 CD; 2 TD; 1 HT	88
CH Cannon River Independence, CD	16 CH; 5 UD; 8 CDX; 21 CD; 1 TDX; 1 TD; 1 NA; 1 HS; 3 PT; 1 HT	136
Select 1 CH Cannon River Oil Tanker, CD	27 CH; 5 CDX; 25 CD; 1 TDX; 1 TD; 1 SH2	133
CH Dieter Vom Konigsberg, CD	18 CH; 1 UD; 7 CDX; 23 CD; 2 TDX; 4 TD	120
CH Donnaj VT Yankee of Paulus, CDX	43 CH; 2 UD; 1 CDX; 31 CD; 2 TD	177
CH Dux Vom Hungerbuhl, SchH I	39 CH; 1 UD; 4 CDX; 15 CD; 2 TD	152
CH Eiko Vom Schwiger Wappen, CDX, SchH III	37 CH; 1 UD; 10 CDX; 32 CD; 6 TD; 1 SH1	188
CH Eppo Von Der Keizerlanden, CDX, BH	13 CH; 3 UD; 6 CDX; 24 CD; 3 TDX; 5 TD; 1 OA; 1 SH1; 1 SH2; 1 SH3; 1 FH;	144
CH Falko Van Het Brabantpark	25 CH; 2 UD; 4 CDX; 15 CD; 2 TDX; 1 TD; 1 SH3	134
CH Gasto Vom Lieberbacherhof, CDX, TD	19 CH; 4 CDX; 21 CD; 1 TD	91
Select CH Goldieche Ara Von Brader, CD	34 CH; 1 UD; 10 CDX; 32 CD; 3 TDX; 2 TD; 1NA; 1 HS; 2 PT; 1 HT	196
Grave Kapenborgh, CD, SchH I	21 CH; 2 UD; 5 CDX; 26 CD; 3 TD; 1 SH2	124
CH Haakon Moby Von Reishoff, CD	13 CH; 1 UD; 6 CDX; 9 CD; 1 TD; 1 NA; 2 PT; 1 HT	77
CH Igor Von Schauer	24 CH; 1 OTCH; 5 CD; 1 TD; 1 SH1	90
Select CH Ironwoods Cade, CD	59 CH; 1 UDX; 3 UD; 5 CDX; 43 CD; 3 PT; 2 HT	261
CH Ironwood Gremlin	26 CH; 2 CDX; 15 CD; 1 TD; 1 PT	101
CH Jack Vom Emstal, CD SchH I	17 CH; 3 CDX; 14 CD; 2 TD	76
CH Kokas K's Degen Von Burga, CD, TD	21 CH; 4 UD; 1 CDX; 5 CD; 1 TD	96
CH Lyn-Mar Acres Arras V Kinta	20 CH; 1 UD; 2 CDX; 7 CD; 1 TD	80

continues

American Rottweiler Club Production Awards as of April 1998 (cont.)

NAME	TITLED OFFSPRING	POINTS
CH McCoy Von Meadow, CD	18 CH; 3 CDX; 13 CD; 2 TD	78
Select CH Mirko Vom Steinkopf, CDX, SchH III	24 CH; 3 UD; 6 CDX; 25 CD; 1 TDX; 1 TD; 3 BH; 1 SH1; 1SH3	153
CH Nelson Van Het Brabantpark	55 CH; 4 CDX; 26 CD; 6 TD; 4 PT	213
Oleo Vom Haus Schmidgall, SchH III, IPO III	9 CH; 1 UD; 3 CDX; 7 CD' 3 TD; 3 SH3; 1 SH2; 1 FH	82
CH Panamint Otso V Kraewel, UD	10 CH; 3 UD; 4 CDX; 6 CD; 6 TD; 1 SH3; 1 SH2; 1 FH	88
CH Pico Vom Hegestrauch, BH, SchH I	19 CH; 1 UD; 2 CDX; 22 CD; 2 TDX; 4 TD; 1 NA; 1 PT; 1 HT; 4 BH; 1 SH1	117
CH Quick Von Siegerhaus, CDX, SchH I	25 CH; 8 CDX; 29 CD; 1 TD; 1 SH1	132
CH Radio Ranch's Axel V Notata	52 CH; 1 UD; 16 CD; 2 TD	180
CH Rodsden's Ansel V Brabant	49 CH; 1 CDX; 11 CD; 1 TD; 1 SH1	165
CH Rodsden's Berte V Zederwald, CDX	39 CH; 1 UD; 9 CDX; 34 CD; 2 TDX; 2 TD; 1 SH1	201
CH Rodsden's Bruin V Hungerbuhl, CDX	51 CH; 2 UD; 4 CDX; 27 CD; 3 TDX; 8 TD	230
CH Rodsden's Elko Kastanienbaum, CDX, TD	31 CH; 8 CDX; 28 CD; 1 TDX; 8 TD; 1 SH3	166
CH Rodsden's Kane V Forstwald, CD	22 CH; 2 CDX; 25 CD; 5 TD; 1 SH1	107
CH Rodsden's Kluge VD Harque, CD	33 CH; 3 UD; 3 CDX; 18 CD; 4 TD; 1 SH2	153
Select CH Tobants Grant	26 CH; 1 UD; 2 CDX; 13 CD; 1 PT; 2 BH	106
CH Trollegen's Fable	16CH; 1 UD; 3 CDX; 16CD	79
CH Trollegen's Frodo, CD	25 CH; 2 UD; 3 CDX; 16 CD; 2 TD	114
CH Von Braders Eiger	11 CH; 1 UD; 6 CDX; 15 CD; 2 TDX; 1 TD	85
CH Von Braders Jem of Phantom WD, UD, TDX	6 CH; 1 CDX; 11 CD; 7 TDX; 6 TD; 1 NA; 4 HT; 5 PT	90
CH Von Gailingen's Matinee Idol, UD, TDX	17 CH; 1 UD; 5 CDX; 13 CD; 1 OA; 4 NA; 3 HS; 6 PT; 1 BH	105
Select CH Von Hottensteins Hubabubba	45 CH; 2 CDX; 9 CD; 1 HS; 6 PT; 3 HT	161
CH Welkerhaus Rommel, UD	17 CH; 2 CDX; 19 CD; 1 TD	77

Gold Dams (45 or more points)

CH Anka Von Gailingen	10 CH; 2 UD; 1 CDX; 5 CD; 2 TD	52
CH Aryan's USS Ursula, CDX, TDX, SchH II	1 CH; 2 UD; 2 TDX; 2 SH3; 2 FH	49
CH Dora VH Kertzenlicht, CD	9 CH; 2 CDX; 12 CD	45
Ebonstern Bryt Promis V Heller	8 CH; 1 UD; 3 CD; 1 TDX; 1 SH2; 1 FH	48
CH Merrymoore's Imp Von Dorow	8 CH; 1 UD; 2 CDX; 6 CD; 1 TDX	48
CH RC's Gator Bel Von Meadow	19 CH; 1 CDX	60

NAME	TITLED OFFSPRING	POINTS
CH Rodsden's Gay Lady, TD	8 CH; 2 CDX; 3 CD; 2 TDX; 2 TD	47
Rodsden's Gypsy	7 CH; 3 UD; 1 CDX; 4 CD; 3 TD	49
CH Rodsden's Heika V Forstwald, CD	6 CH; 2 CDX; 6 CD; 6 BH; 1 SH3; 1 SH1	46
CH Rodsden's Lady Luck, CD	12 CH; 1 UD; 2 CD; 1 TD; 1 SH1	50
CH Rodsden's Sun-Burst Truffa, CDX, TDX, PT	4 CH; 1 UDX; 2 UD; 2 CDX; 5 CD; 1 TDX; 2 TD; 2 NA; 1 PT	55
CH Seren's Just Dazzling Zanne, CDX	5 CH; 2 UDX; 1 UD; 1 CDX; 5 CD;	47
Select 1 CH Sophe Von Bergenhof, CDX	9 CH; 1 UD; 4 CDX; 2 CD; 4 TD; 1 PT	52
CH Stefen Sadie VH Kertzenlicht, CD, TD	1 CH; 3 UDX; 2 TDX; 1 TD; 1 OA; 1 BH; 1 SH2; 1 FH	56
Select 1 CH Tri-Lee's Champagne, CD	10 CH; 3 CDX; 9 CD; 2 TD; 1 BH	52
CH V Gailingen's Welkerhaus CIA, CD	9 CH; 1 CDX; 14 CD; 1 TD	45
CH Wilderness Kasha, CD	6 CH; 1 UD; 2 CDX; 10 CD; 5 BH; 1 PT	46
Wyvonie Van Het Brabantpark, CD, TD	4 CH; 1 UD; 1 CDX; 6 CD; 1 TDX; 1 TD; 2 SH3; 1 FH	52

Rottweilers That Have Earned the AKC Utility Excellent Title (UDX)

Cammcastle's Able Warlock, UDX
Dog bred by S. Cain
Owned by L. Catlett

Yana Von Siegerhaus, UDX
Bitch bred by C. and T. Woodward
Owned by M. and R. Belardinelli

OTCH Elsa S Geer, UDX
Bitch bred by B. Burke
Owned by C. and J. Geer

Amazing Grace III, UDX
Bitch bred by M. Farmer
Owned by A. Johnson

SAF Grandee of Demara, UDX
Bitch bred by B. and S. Spooner
Owned by R. and M. Bellardinelli and B. and
S. Spooner

Baron Nikolas, UDX, TDX
Dog bred by S. Quick
Owned by J. Klingner

OTCH Rock Solid Risky Business, UDX
Bitch bred by W. Harris
Owned by B. Kiefer

Bevrons Krusader v Stefen, UDX
Dog bred by J. and W. Stevens
Owned by R. and B. Koldon

Walking H Admrl V Quicksilver, UDX
Dog bred and owned by D. Holmes

Sun-Burst Miss Nellie Bly, UDX, TDX
Bitch bred by R. DeSalvio
Owned by E. and S. Dupont

- Tealska Leader of the Pack, UDX, NA
  Dog bred by S. Potter and S. Grohs
  Owned by R. Bizer

- CH West Winds Ayla, UDX
  Bitch bred and owned by A. Seitz

- Nordikes Gotcha Going Levi, UDX, NA
  Dog bred by N. Dikeman
  Owned by E. Swancer

- Rodsden's Jorgen V Quira, UDX
  Dog bred by R. Maloney and S. Rademacher
  Owned by J. Sebert

- Kristopher Carl K C, UDX, OA
  Dog bred by H. and R. Weishaar
  Owned by B. and S. Barkus

- Stefen Imzadie's Hannelore, UDX, TDX, OA
  Bitch bred by J. and W. Stevens
  Owned by M. Blenz

- Cammcastle's Funando Gotcha, UDX
  Dog bred by S. Cain
  Owned by L. Catlett

- Ul Malia Aloha, UDX
  Bitch of unknown breeding
  Owned by C. and H. Livingston

American Rottweiler Club Versatility Excellent Awards

The Versatility Excellent (VX) title is awarded to dogs who have distinguished themselves by earning an advanced degree in Obedience (CDX) or Schutzhund (SchH I). Additionally, the recipients of the VX must demonstrate the ability to perform at the highest levels by accumulating at least six points in a single working category (Obedience, Schutzhund, Tracking, Herding or Agility).

- A minimum of 14 points must be earned.

- A Versatility (V) award must have been earned.

- At least 3 of the required points must come from Obedience or Schutzhund.

- At least 6 of the required points must come from a single working category, not a combination of working categories.

- No more than 3 points may come from miscellaneous.

VX Award-Winning Rottweilers

Magnum Vom Falconhurst, UD, TDX, SchH III,   27
FH, IPO III, DPO III
   A. Slaughter

Black Oaks Briana Vom Mt Olympus,   26
UD, tDX, SchH III, FH, WH
   A. Slaughter

CH Seren's Atomahowk of Neshobe, CDX, TDX, SchH III, FH, BH, CGC, TDI, Ztpr   26
    M. and P. Piusz

CH Blitz Vom Van Haus, UD, TD, SchH III, FH, BH, CGC   23
    J. Noble

Arnie Vom Bruhlhof, CDX, SchH III, FH, CGC   20
    L. Bzdon

Dardon's Justin Tyme V Stefen, CDX, tDX, SchH I, BH, CGC   18
    D. Wielert

CH Mirko Vom Steinkopf, CDX, SchH III, FH, IPO III   18
    R. and R. Wayburn

A/C CH Von Gailingen's Matinee Idol, UD, TDX, HIC, AgI, CGC   18
    C. Thompson

CH Von Braders Jem of Phantom WD, UD, TDX, CGC   17
    K. Ebert

A/C CH Birch Hill's Ringmaster, UD, TDX, TT   16
    S. Voorhees

CH Birch Hill's Warwick, CDX, TDX, SchH I, CGC   16
    J. Wiedel

Dumarz Vom Haus Slaughter, CD, TD, BH, SchH III, FH, WH   16
    S. Slaughter

CH Axel VD Marorie, CDX, SchH I, BH, CGC, TDI, TT, Ztpr   15
    D. LePage and G. Daigle

Kasie A Golden West, UD, TDX, HIC, CGC   15
    M. Kemper

CH Rodsden's Sun-Burst Truffa, CDX, TDX, PT, BH, CGC   15
    R. DiSalvio

CH Winterhawk's Chief Justice, UD, TD, SchH I, VB, TT   15
    C. and J. Justice

Baron Nikolas, UD, TDX, BH, CGC   14
    J. Klinger

Baron OJ Von Yden, Ud, SchH I, VB, HIC, TT, CGC, TDI   14
    D. LePage and G. Daigle

OTCH Dolly Vom Odenwald, TD, SchH I, CGC, TT   14
    A. Summers

Frolicn's Dillon V Edelhart, UD, BH, HI, CGC   14
    P. Frost

Gewitters Argus, UD, TDX, BH, TT   14
    P. Novosad

CH Starshine's Anna Katrine, CDX, HT, PT, HI, CGC, TDI   14
    J. Benson

Stechpalme's Desperado, UD, TDX, HIC, TT   14
    T. Millsap

Stefen's Imzadie's Hanelore, UD   14
    M. Blenz

OTCH Summers Glory Da Bratianan, HT, BH, CGC, TDI, Carting II   14
    A. Summers

CH Tealaska Ringmaster's Esprit, CDX, TDX   14
    S. Voorhees

Von Bruka Bewitched, UDX, NA, BH, HIC, CGC   14
    J. Burkhardt

CH West Winds Ayla, UDX, BH, CGC   14
    A. Seitz

Specialty Winners

1987 ARC National Specialty—Pasadena, Texas

Best of Breed	Select 1 CH Cannon River Oil Tanker, CD
Best of Opposite Sex	Select 1 Cendy Vom Siedlerpfad
Selects	Select CH Dachmar's Fascination (B)
	Select CH Goldeiche Ara Von Brader, CD
	Select CH Mirko Vom Steinkopf
	Select CH Von Bruka Fiona, CD (B)
Obedience High in Trial	OTCH Dolly Vom Odenwald, TD, SchH I
Schutzhund High in Trial	Barry vom Lohlein, SchH III

1988 ARC National Specialty—Oakland, California

Best of Breed   Select 1 CH Cannon River Oil Tanker, CD

Best of Opposite Sex   Select 1 CH Sophe Von Bergenhof, CD

Selects   Select CH Eischenwalds Basil V Axel

                                 Select CH Goldeiche Ara Von Brader, CD

                                 Select CH Obstgartens Countess Oraya (B)

                                 Select CH Tanmar Beaverbrook Bess (B)

                                 Select CH Vom Sonnenhaus Krugerrand

Obedience High in Trial   Summers Glory Da Bratiana, CD

Schutzhund High in Trial   Barry Vom Lohlein, SchH III

1989 ARC National Specialty—Hamilton, Ohio

Best of Breed   Select 1 CH Vom Sonnenhaus Krugerrand, CD

Best of Opposite Sex   Select 1 CH Tri-Lee's Champagne

Selects   Select Boss of Hale's Hollow

                                 Select CH Goldeiche Ara Von Brader, CD

                                 Select CH Ironwoods Cade

                                 Select CH Legend's Invocation (B)

                                 Select CH Von Riddle's Gabriel V Eisen, CD (B)

                                 Select CH Windwalkers Ada Von Mirko (B)

                                 Select CH Wisterias Bismark V Fruhling, CD

Obedience High in Trial   Summers Glory Da Bratiana, CD

Schutzhund High in Trial   CH Liberty's A Chip Off the Ark, CDX, SchH III

1990 ARC National Specialty—Knoxville, Tennessee

Best of Breed   Select 1 CH Cannon River Oil Tanker, CD

Best of Opposite Sex   Select 1 CH Jessnic's Marvelous Mamie Cade

Selects	Select CH Boss VD Biestse Hoeve, CD
	Select CH Goldeiche Ara Von Brader, CD
	Select CH Grunhaus Harmony Marie, CD (B)
	Select CH Mr. Impressive of Helkirk
	Select CH Rodsden's Cossack Von Brader, CD
	Select CH Vom Sonnenhaus Krugerrand, CD
	Select CH Von Brader's Icelander
	Select CH Von Bruka Indra V Yden, CDX (B)
Obedience High in Trial	Welkerhaus' Gutherzig Bear, CD
Schutzhund High in Trial	Dingo Von Der Lichten Ade, SchH III

1991 ARC National Specialty—Bothell, Washington

Best of Breed	Select 1 CH Von Der Lors Anastashia Cade (B)
Best of Opposite Sex	Select 1 CH Beaverbrook Phantom V Rika
Selects	Select CH Don-Ari's Harras
	Select CH Nighthawk's Commotion (B)
	Select CH Tri-Lee's Down The Road, TD (B)
	Select CH Von Hottensteins Hubabubba
Obedience High in Trial	OTCH Carla Vom Kasseler Hof

1992 ARC National Specialty—Boxborough, Massachusetts

Best of Breed	Select 1 CH Gamegards Image De Femme (B)
Best of Opposite Sex	Select 1 CH Akemo's Apache Von Godhart
Selects	Select CH Bandera's Lili Marlene V Lore (B)
	Select CH Noblehaus Klark Kent
	Select CH Pioneer's DJ Star Stuben, CD
	Select CH Von Der Lors Anastashia Cade (B)
	Select CH Von Heizermans Avenging Angel (B)
Obedience High in Trial	Starshine's Astra

1993 ARC National Specialty—San Jose, California

Best of Breed	Select 1 Black Oak Chance V Coldar, CD
Best of Opposite Sex	Select 1 CH Tri-Lee's Gypsy Arabesque
Selects	Select CH Bandera's Brock Von Brando
	Select CH Hi Sierra Dozer of Burton
	Select CH Imaygo's Midnight Cruiser, CD
	Select CH Tobant's Grant
	Select CH Tri-Lee's Fatal Attraction, CD (B)
	Select CH Von Der Lors Dare Desperado (B)
Obedience High in Trial	Rubicons Mad Max

1994 ARC National Specialty—North Canton, Ohio

Best of Breed	Select 1 CH Oakbrook Caliber V Doroh
Best of Opposite Sex	Select 1 CH Rivera's Anka
Selects	Select CH Andrecas Aramis Von Der Mond, CD
	Select CH Corinthian's Heart Breaker
	Select CH Gamegards Half Moon (B)
	Select CH Gamegards Moonraker
	Select CH Legends Dark Invocation (B)
	Select CH Vom Lida's Dragonz Treasure
	Select CH Wildwood's Shelby Von Wehner (B)
Obedience High in Trial	Summers Glory Da Bratiana, UD

1995 ARC National Specialty—Perry, Georgia

Best of Breed	Select 1 CH Dillon Von Wacissa, CD
Best of Opposite Sex	Select 1 CH Noblehaus High C V Gruppstark, CD
Selects	Select CH Andrecas Aramis Von Der Mond, CD
	Select CH Fine's Ciara Von Covenant (B)
	Select CH Nighthawk's Go for the Gold (B)
	Select CH Serrant's Bannor
	Select CH Tri-Lee's Grand Finale (B)
	Select CH Vom Lida's Dragonz Treasure
	Select CH Windrock's Jack Hammer
Obedience High in Trial	Eichenbergs Black Diamond

1996 ARC National Specialty—Bremerton, Washington

Best of Breed	Select 1 CH Serrants Bannor
Best of Opposite Sex	Select 1 CH Von Boylands Boldly Bridgette, CD
Selects	Select CH Degrassos Jacob V Waxel
	Select CH Farwest's Barritz V Lundhaus, CD (B)
	Select CH Full Moon's As Good Asit Gets
	Select CH Mako Von Der Bleichstrasse
	Select CH Mar-Gra Ferrari Von Helken, CD
	Select CH Wittz Jamaica Breeze, CD (B)
Obedience High in Trial	Valley View Election Day
Herding High in Trial	Taj's Alluring Demi Von Zaber

1997 ARC National Specialty—Lima, Ohio

Best of Breed	Select 1 CH Champ Vom Vilstalerland
Best of Opposite Sex	Select 1 CH Jeneck's Noonka
Selects	Select CH Asgard's Call Girl of Aqua (B)
	Select CH Evrmor's U R the One
	Select CH Gamegards Moonraker
	Select CH Goldwind's Lindy V Myers, CD (B)
	Select CH Highline A Natural Attraction
	Select CH Highline Allusive Dream (B)
	Select CH Indian Ridge's Apache V Epic
	Select CH Von Hottensteins Up an Atem (B)
	Select CH Windrock's Jack Hammer
Obedience High in Trial	CH Rubicon's Sud'N Impact-Crash, CD
Herding High in Trial	SAF Quaint Thera Tee, PT

1998 ARC National Specialty—Plano, Texas

Best of Breed	Select 1 CH Degrassos Jacob V Waxel, CD
Best of Opposite Sex	Select 1 CH Farwest's Barritz Von Lundhaus
Selects	Select CH Abby Vom Schwaiger Wappen (B)
	Select CH Andreca's Aramis Von Der Mond, CDX
	Select CH Crystal's Topaz V Ponca
	Select CH Gamegards Moonraker
	Select CH Mount Olympus Cartels Exacta
	Select CH Rampart's King's Ransom
	Select CH Rubicon's Sud'N Impact-Crash, CD
	Select CH Sampson's Anna Belle Cadence (B)
	Select CH Vom Hochfeld's Seminole Wind (B)
Obedience High in Trial	Tealaska Leader of the Pack, UDX, OA
Herding High in Trial	A/C CH Buddenhaus Babe V Siegerhaus, CD
Agility High in Trial	Jailbird's Governor's Pardon, NA

The Thompson wHELPing Box

This Thompson wHELPing Box design first appeared in the January/February 1976 ARK newsletter. It has been copied and adapted many times since its original publication. Puppy owners who have purchased puppies from breeders who have used this design have been very grateful for the ease of housebreaking a puppy whose natural instincts to not soil his den have been reinforced since birth. This is Greg and Cathy's original design and commentary.

We strongly suggest the potty wall; it has worked out great and makes cleaning up a snap. We kept the larger compartment carpeted, while we covered the smaller with a thick layer of newspaper and topped it with shredded newspaper.

We built this box to fit a specific space and also so that it could be taken down and stored inside itself.

Other suggestions: Make the box bigger if you can—four by eight feet is a much better size—and add pig rails. You can make pig rails by using two-by-fours supported by four-inch pieces of two-by-twos.

We used two-by-fours for the floor frame, but two-by-twos would be just as good. The side walls, potty wall and gate slides were made of half-inch plywood. The heavier the grade of plywood for the floor, the better.

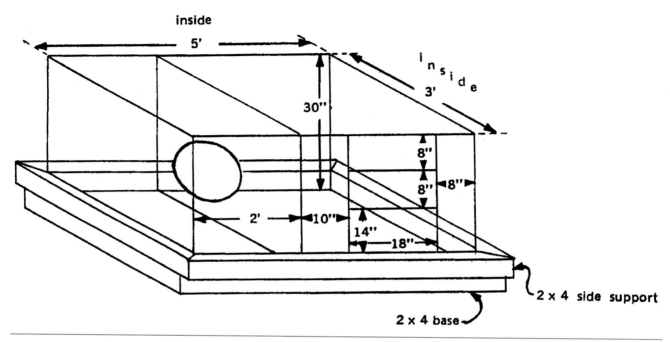

Dimensions of the Thompson WHELPing Box. Note the 30-inch sides. These are higher than most to accommodate puppies up to twelve weeks old.

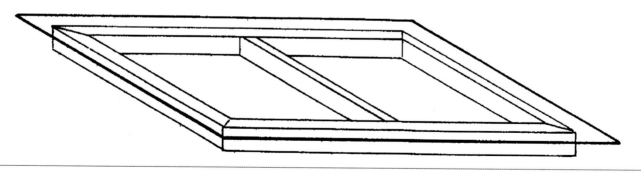

Schematic representation of the base.

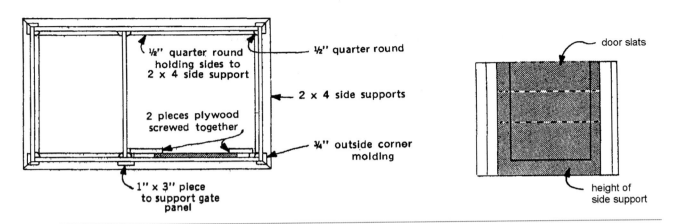

Quarter rounds are placed inside base to provide additional support for the walls. Door slats are different heights so that as the puppies grow they won't crawl or climb out.

The base for the floor can be either two-by-fours or two-by-twos. It does not matter whether the corners are mitered. The floor then is screwed to the base, and the side support two-by-fours are screwed on to support the side walls. Remember that the thickness of these two-by-fours and the thickness of the plywood walls are in addition to the inside dimensions of the box.

The door can be moved to either end to suit your room layout. It will be stronger if you do not cut the front side all the way down.

We like the slatted door so that the bitch can jump in and out, and it can be raised as the puppies grow, but a hinged door is fine.

The sides are held against the two-by-four side support by a half-inch quarter round screwed or nailed to the floor. The potty wall is also held up by a half-inch quarter round nailed or screwed to the walls. The potty wall hole should be cut low enough for four-week-old puppies to go over and large enough for eight- to ten-week-old puppies to fit through.

Finishing nails were used to hold the corner molding to the walls, but deck screws or long screws are better.

Bibliography

ROTTWEILER BOOKS

The Basic Guide to the Rottweiler. Edited by Michael R. Zervas. Virginia: Dace Publishing, 1996.

Blackmore, Joan. *A Dog Owner's Guide to the Rottweiler.* New Jersey: Tetra Press, 1987.

Brace, Andrew. *The Ultimate Rottweiler.* New York: Howell Book House, 1995.

Churchill, Janet. *Rottweiler.* Virginia: Denlingers Publishing Ltd., 1998.

Elsden, Judy and Larry Elsden. *The Rottweiler Today.* New York: Howell Book House, 1992.

Freeman, Muriel. *The Complete Rottweiler.* New York: Howell Book House, 1984.

Hodinar, Dagmar. *The Rottweiler: An International Study of the Breed.* New Jersey: Von Palisaden Publications, 1985.

Klem, Joan R. and Susan C. Rademacher. *The Rottweiler Experience.* New York: Howell Book House, 1996.

Macphail, Mary. *All About the Rottweiler.* London: Pelham Books Ltd., 1986.

Pettengell, Jim. *The New Rottweiler.* New Jersey: TFH, 1995.

Price, Les. *Rottweilers: An Owners Companion.* New York: Howell Book House, 1991.

The Rottweiler Annual. Edited by Cynthia L. Kerstiens. Colorado: Hoflin Publishing, Inc., 1993–97.

The Rottweiler Pictorial, 4th and 5th ed. Edited by Catherine M. Thompson. American Rottweiler Club, 1987 and 1994.

Stratton, Richard F. *The Rottweiler.* New Jersey: TFH, 1985.

PAMPHLETS AVAILABLE FROM THE AMERICAN KENNEL CLUB

The following educational/instructional pamphlets are available free of charge by writing to: American Kennel Club, Customer Service, 5580 Centerview Dr., Raleigh NC, 27606-3390.

Agility Regulations

Herding Regulations

Guidelines for Dog Show Judges

Guidelines for Obedience Judges

Obedience Regulations

Rules Applying to Dog Shows

Tracking Regulations

GENERAL INFORMATION

Baer, Nancy and Steve Duno. *Leader of the Pack: How to Take Control of Your Relationship with Your Dog.* Harper Mass Market Paperbacks, 1996.

Barwig, Susan. *Schutzhund: Theory and Training Methods.* New York: Howell Book House, 1991.

Benjamin, Carol Lea. *Dog Problems: A Professional Trainer's Guide.* New York: Howell Book House, 1989.

——. *Second Hand Dog: How to Turn Yours into a First Rate Pet.* New York: Howell Book House, 1996.

Benjamin, Carol Lea and Stephen Lennard. *Mother Knows Best: The Natural Way to Train Your Dog.* New York: Howell Book House, 1985.

——. *Surviving Your Dog's Adolescence: A Positive Training Program.* New York: Howell Book House, 1993.

Craige, Patricia. *Born to Win: Breed to Succeed.* Oregon: Doral Publishing, 1997.

Daniels, Julie. *Enjoying Dog Agility: From Backyard to Competition.* Oregon: Doral Publishing, 1991.

Dildei, Gottfried and Sheila Booth. *Schutzhund Obedience: Training in Drive.* Podium Publications, 1992.

Fisher, John. *Dogwise: The Natural Way to Train Your Dog.* London: Souvenier Press Ltd., 1996.

Gilbert, Edward M., Curtice M. Brown, and Thelma R. Brown. *K-9 Structure and Terminology.* New York: Howell Book House, 1995.

Hogan, Julie and Donna Thompson. *Practical Tracking for Practically Anyone.* 1995.

Holst, Phyllis. *Canine Reproduction.* Colorado: Alpine Publications, 1985.

Johnson, Glen R. *Tracking Dog: Theory and Methods.* New York: Arner Publications, 1975.

Kilcommons, Brian and Paul Kunkel. *Good Owners Great Dogs.* Warner Books, 1992.

Kilcommons, Brian and Sarah Wilson. *Childproofing Your Dog: A Complete Guide to Preparing Your Dog for the Children in Your Life.* Warner Books, 1994.

Pryor, Karen. *Don't Shoot the Dog.* New York: Bantam Books, 1984.

Rutherford, Clarice and David H. Neil. *How to Raise a Puppy You Can Live With.* Colorado: Alpine Publications, 1992.

Simmons-Moake, Jane. *Agility Training: The Fun Sport for All Dogs.* New York: Howell Book House, 1993.

MULTIMEDIA

The Rottweiler CD. Sherluck MultiMedia, 29001 176th Ave. SE, Kent, WA 98042.

MAGAZINES

Breed Specific Rottweiler. 121 Weathervane Dr. Cherry Hill, NJ 08002.

The Rottweiler Perspective. P.O. Box 550. Brownsburg, Quebec, Canada, J0V 1A0.

The Rottweiler Quarterly. P.O. Box 900. Aromas, CA 95004.

VIDEOS

Elliot, Rachel Paige. *Dog Steps.* American Kennel Club.

Herding. Canine Training Systems.

In the Ribbons Rottweiler. Canine Training Systems.

Klem, Joan R. *Let's Talk About Rottweilers.* JRK Videos.

——. *The Ultimate Rottweiler.* Canine Training Systems.

The Rottweiler. American Kennel Club.

Silverton, Annemarie. *Competitive Obedience.* Canine Training Systems.

Simmons-Moake, Jane. *Competitive Agility Training.* Canine Training Systems.

WEB SITE ADDRESSES

American Kennel Club
www.akc.org

American Rottweiler Club
www.amrottclub.org

National Animal Poison Control Center
www.napcc.aspca.org

Index

A

Adolescence, 48–51
Adopting older dogs, 34–35
ADRK (Allgemeiner Deutscher
    Rottweiler Klub), 9–10, 15, 20,
    164–65
Agility events, 95–96
Aging. *See* Older Rottweilers
Allergies, 64
Allgemeiner Deutscher Rottweiler
    Klub (ADRK), 9–10, 15, 20,
    164–65
American Herding Breeds
    Association (AHBA), 97, 153
American Kennel Club (AKC), 9
    AKC Events Calendar, 80, 153
    AKC Gazette, 153

breed standard, 10, 15–27
breeder referral line, 35, 37
breeding rules, 119
Home Again microchip
    program, 40
local Rottweiler clubs and, 145
performance events, 92–97
Rottweiler champions, 105–9
American Rottweiler Club (ARC),
    10, 15, 35, 145–49, 153
breeder referral service, 148
mandatory practices, 157–59
National Specialty, 146–48, 175–80
production awards, 167–71
specialty shows, 146
Web site, 105, 148
American Temperament Test Society
    (ATTS), 154

Anatolian, 6
Antihistamine, 64
Appenzeller, 8
Arthritis, 134, 138
Artificial insemination, 124
Australian Shepherd Club of
    America (ASCA), 97, 154

B

Babies, 44–45
Bailey, Carlton, 13
Bait, 82
Balls, choking and, 61
Bathing, 76–77
Behavior, breed standard, 27
Benadryl, 64
Bernese Mountain Dog, 8

Bitches, breeding
  boarding, 121–22
  evaluating, 116–17, 120–21, 131
  mating, 125–26
  medical tests required, 127
  muzzle for, 124–25
  receptivity, 123–24
  whelping, 181–83
Bite
  breed standard, 18, 27
  checking before breeding, 120
  judge's inspection of, 85
Boars, hunting, 8
Boredom, signs of, 2
Bowls, 48
Breed seminars, 27
Breed standard. See Standard, breed
Breeders
  distinguished, 108
  guarantees of, 33
  responsibilities of, 30–35, 116–17,
    128–30, 157–59
  sales contracts with, 32–33
  showing your dog and, 80, 88
Breeding, 111–30
  ARC mandatory practices,
    157–59
  bitches. See Bitches, breeding
  costs of, 115–16, 128
  deciding whether to breed,
    112–18
  the mating, 123–27
  placing puppies, 129
  record-keeping requirements,
    113–14
  risks and rewards, 129–30
  studs, 117–27
Bronze Age, 6
Brucellosis test, 118

Brushing, 73, 138–39
Butchers, Rottweiler and, 7–8

C

Canine Eye Registration
  Foundation (CERF), 154
Cardiopulmonary resuscitation
  (CPR), 61–62
Cars, heatstroke and, 62–63
Carting, 97
Celebrities, Rottweilers and, 12
Children, 32, 43–45
Choke collars, 48
Choking, 60–61
Classified ads, 30–31, 37
Clipping nails, 74
Coat, 2, 73
  breed standard, 21–22, 27
Collar, 47–48
Colonial Rottweiler Club, 10
Color, breed standard, 22–23, 27
Companion Dog titles, 92, 162
Companions, Rottweilers as,
  40–42
Corneal ulcers, 66
CPR (cardiopulmonary
  resuscitation), 61–62
Crates, 47, 54–55
Crestwood Kennel, 11

D

Day, Alexandra, 13, 43
Death, planning for, 142
Dehydration
  in older Rottweilers, 137
  in puppies, 129
  signs of, 64

Dentition, 19
  judge's inspection of, 85
Desexing, 51
Deutscher Verband der
  Gebrauchshundsportvereine
  (DVG), 101
Dewclaws, 21
Diabetes, 135
Diarrhea, 63–64
Diet, 53–54, 70. See also Feeding
  for old Rottweilers, 135–36
Directed jumping exercise, 94
Directed retrieve exercise, 93–94
Disabilities, people with, 101
Disqualifying faults, 18–19, 22–23,
  26–27
Dodge, Geraldine Rockefeller,
  11, 13
Dog Fancy, 154
Dog shows. See also Performance
  events; Showing your
  Rottweiler
  contacting breeders at, 37
Dog World, 154
Doherty, Shannon, 13
Draft work, 8, 97
Dry baths, 77

E

Ears
  breed standard, 18–19
  care of, 56, 71, 75–76
  checking, 138–39
  hearing loss, 134
Eclampsia, 128
Eichler, Arthur Alfred, 10
Entlebucher, 8
Entropion, 18, 27, 66–67

Equipment, 47–48
Estrus, 73, 127–28
Euthanasia, 140–42
Exercise, 70–71
  for older Rottweilers, 137–38
Expression, breed standard, 18
Eyes
  breed standard, 18–19
  problems, 66
  sight loss, 134

F

Famous Rottweilers, 103, 167–80
Faults, 27
  in coat, 22–23
  in general appearance, 17
  in head, 18–19
Federation Cynologic
    Internationale (FCI), 15,
    19–27
Feeding, 53–54
  old Rottweilers, 135–36
  puppies, 70, 129
  treats, 41–42, 82, 136
Feet, checking, 138
Fetch, 71, 138
Fighting dogs, in Rottweiler
    ancestry, 8
First aid kit, 59–60
Flea baths, 77
Fleas, 57
Flyball, 97–98
Follow Me Kennel, 11
Ford, Benson, 13
Forequarters, breed standard,
    18–20
Freeger Kennel, 11
Freeman, Mrs. Bernard, 10, 11

G

Gait(ing), 80, 84, 86
  breed standard, 23–25
Games, 45–47, 71, 138
General appearance, breed
    standard, 17
German Stud Book (ADRK), 9
Giralda Kennel, 11
Golden State Rottweiler Club, 10
Good Dog Carl books (Alexandra
    Day), 13, 43
Great Pyrenees, 6
Greater Swiss Mountain Dog, 8, 20
Grief counseling, 140
Griffey, Ken, Jr., 13
Grooming, 2, 73–77
  older Rottweilers, 138–39
Grosvenor, Melville Bell, 7
Growing pains, 66
Growling, 49
Guarantees, in sales contracts, 33
Guard dogs, demand for, 11
Guide dogs, Rottweilers as, 101

H

Handlers, professional, 86–89
Handling, daily, 42–43
Handling classes, 80
Hardaway, Penny, 13
Head, breed standard, 18–19
Health care, 53–66
  allergies, 64
  choking, 60–61
  CPR, 61–62
  crates, 54–55
  diarrhea, 63–64, 66

encounters with wild animals,
    64–65
  feeding, 53–54
  first vet visit, 56
  fleas, 57
  heatstroke, 62–63
  inoculation schedule, 56
  poisoning, 58–60
  puppy proofing your home, 58
  red flags, 66–67
  tapeworms, 57
  ticks, 58
  vomiting, 63
Health certificates, 30, 67, 118,
    120, 127
Health checks, before purchase, 30
Hearing loss, 134
Heart problems, 66
Heartworm, 56
Heatstroke, 62–63, 134
Heid, Herman, 11
Heimlich maneuver, 60–61
Herding events, 96–97
Hindquarters, 21
Hip dysplasia, 33, 66, 134
History of the Rottweiler, 5–13
  ancient, 6, 7, 8
  clubs, 9
  early champions, 10–11
  evolution, 6
  famous owners, 12–13
  mixed ancestry, 8–9
  name, 7–8
  popularity, 11–12
  in the United States, 10
Hoard, Barbara, 11
Home Again microchip
    program, 40
Hot spots, 57

Housebreaking, 55, 69
Hunting dogs, in Rottweiler
ancestry, 8

I

ID tags, 40
Inoculation schedule, 56
Insurance companies, 2, 12
International Friends of the
Rottweiler, 20
International Weight Pull
Association (IWPA), 154
Internet, the
ARC Web Site, 148
contacting breeders on, 37
grief counseling through, 140

J

Jones, Noel Paul, 11
Judges, in breed shows, 83–86

K

Kennel dog syndrome, 35
Kennels, 11
Knecht, August, 9, 11
Komondor, 6
Kuvasz, 6

L

Lameness, 66
Landesverband DVG America
(Schutzhund), 155
Leashes, 48
Limping, 66
Lindenwood bloodline, 11

Lips, breed standard, 18–19
Luburich, Felice, 11
Lyme disease, 58

M

Madden, John, 13
Male Rottweilers
adolescence, 48–51
neutering, 51
Marema, 6
Massengill douche, 65
Mastiff, Tibetan, 6
Mastitis, 129
Matches, 81
Mating, 123–27
Medallion Rottweiler Club, 10
Microchips for identification, 40, 159
Mollosus, 6
Mondale, Walter, 13
Mounting behaviors, 49
Mouth, breed standard, 27
Muzzle (anatomy), breed standard,
18–19
Muzzle (restraint), 124–25

N

Nails, clipping, 56, 74, 138–39
National Association for Search and
Rescue (NASAR), 155
National Dog Registry, 155
Neck, breed standard, 19
Neutering, 51
in sales contracts, 33
North American Dog Agility Club
(NADAC), 97
North American Dog Agility
Council (NADAC), 155

North American Flyball Association
(NAFA), 155
Nutrition. See also Diet; Feeding
for old Rottweilers, 135–36

O

Obedience events, 92–94
Obedience Trial Champion title,
92, 94
Rottweiler winners, 108
Obesity
in older Rottweilers, 134–35
in puppies, 54
OCD (osteochondrosis
dessecans), 66
OFA hip certification, 157–58
OFA hip clearance, 33
OFA (Orthopedic Foundation for
Animals), 30
Older Rottweilers, 133–42
adopting, 34–35
aging process, 133–35
diet, 135–36
drinking habits, 137
euthanasia, 140
exercise, 137–38
grooming, 138–39
other pets and, 139–40
routine for, 135
O'Neal, Shaquille, 13
Orthopedic Foundation for Animals
(OFA), 30, 155
Osteochondrosis dessecans
(OCD), 66
Other pets, older Rottweilers and,
139–40
Owens, Buck, 13

P–Q

Palos Park Kennel, 11
Panamint Kennel, 11
Panoesteitis, 66
Parasites, external, 57–58
Paul, Adrian, 13
Pedigrees, 33–34
  terms found in, 166
Performance events, 91–101
  agility, 95–96
  draft work, 97
  flyball, 97–98
  herding, 96–97
  obedience, 92–94
  schutzhund, 98–101
  tracking, 94–95
Pinkerton, Erna, 11
Pinkett, Jada, 13
Pippin, Scottie, 13
Play, 71
Poisoning, 58
Police work, Rottweilers in, 9, 101
Porcupines, 64
Preeclampsia, 129
Production awards, ARC, 167–71
Professional Handlers Association
    (PHA), 88
Professional Handlers Guild
    (PHG), 88
Proportion, breed standard, 17–18
Puppies
  choking and, 60
  collars for, 47
  crates for, 56
  exercise, 70–71
  feeding, 53–54, 129
  handling classes for, 80
  hip dysplasia and, 66

housebreaking, 55, 69
poisoning and, 58
raising, 128
selecting. *See* Selecting a
    Rottweiler
showing, 81–83
socialization of, 43, 129
veterinarians and, 56
viral and bacterial infections, 66
Puppy proofing your home, 58

R

Rabies, 61
Registration papers, 34
Rescue groups, 35
Responsible ownership, 3, 70–71,
    130, 140, 151
Retrieving, 71
Reynolds, Burt, 13
Rice, Jerry, 13
Rocky Mountain Spotted
    Fever, 58
Rodsden Kennel, 11
Roman army, 6, 7
Rostad, Wayne, 13
Rottweil (Germany), 7–8
Rottweiler, origin of name, 7
Routine, for old Rottweilers, 135

S

Safety, 3
Sales contracts with breeders, 32–33
Sanders, Deion, 13
SAS (subaortic stenosis), 66
Scent discrimination exercise, 93
Schoelkopf, Eugene, 11
Schutzhund, 98–101

Search and rescue work, 101
Selecting a Rottweiler, 29–37
  breeders and, 31–32, 37
  classified ads, 30–31, 37
  health considerations, 30
  pedigrees, 33
  registration papers, 34–35
  rescue groups, 35
  sales contracts, 32
  sex, 35
Sennenhunds, 8, 9
Severinson, Doc, 12–13
Sex characteristics, 17, 27,
    35–37, 51
Shedding, 73
Sheep, 6
Show prospects, purchasing, 33
Showing your Rottweiler, 79–88
  the big show, 82–86
  entering a show, 81–82
  learning, 80–81
  professional handlers, 86–89
Sight loss, 134
Signal exercise, 92–93
Size, 45
  breed standard, 17–18
Skunk-Off, 65
Skunks, 64
Slip collars. *See* Choke collars
Smith, Will, 13
Socialization, 43
  of puppies, 129
Spaying, 51
Specialty winners, 175–80
Sperm, freezing and storage of,
    126–27
Srigo Kennels, 11, 13
Stacking, 80, 84, 86
Stahl, William, 11

Standard, breed
  ADRK, 9
  American Kennel Club (1990),
    15–27
  coat, 21–22, 27
  color, 22–23, 27
  disqualifications (faults), 18–19,
    22–23, 26–27
  ears, 18–19
  eyes, 18–19
  first American, 10
  forequarters, 18–20
  gait, 23–25
  general appearance, 17
  head, 18–19
  hindquarters, 21
  neck, topline, 19
  size, proportion, 17–18
  substance, 17, 19
  temperament, 24–26
Stealing of Rottweilers, 39–40
Stina vom Felsenmeer, 9
Stock guardians, 6
Studs, 117–27
  information packs on, 118–19
  medical tests required, 118
  stud contracts, 119
Subaortic stenosis (SAS), 66
Substance, breed standard, 17–18
Supplements, 136–37
  imming, 71, 138
  zerland, farm dogs in, 8

T

9–20, 129

Tapeworms, 57
Tattooing for identification, 40, 159
Teeth
  breed standard, 18–19, 27
  brushing, 56, 74
  cleaning, 138–39
Temperament, 1–3
  breed standard, 24–26
Theft of Rottweilers, 39–40
Therapy Dogs International, 155
Therapy work, 98
Thompson, Catherine, 10
Thompson wHELPing Box,
  181–83
Tibetan Mastiff, 6
Ticks, 58
Tie (mating), 126
Tikka, Elvi, 5–13
Topline, breed standard, 19
Toys, 45–47, 71, 138
Tracking, 94–95
Training, impromptu, 41
Training classes, 43, 51
Traveling with a Rottweiler, 55
Treats, 41–42, 136
  bait, 82
Tug-of-war, 45–47, 138

U

United Kennel Club, 97, 155
United Schutzhund Clubs of
  America (USA), 99, 155
United States Dog Agility
  Association (USDAA), 97
United States Rottweiler Club
  (USRC), 99

U. S. Dog Agility Association
  (USDAA), 155
Utility Dog titles, 92–94, 171

V

Valium, 142
Versatility awards, 149, 172–74
Veterinarians
  euthanasia and, 140–42
  first visit to, 56, 66
  inoculation schedule, 56
  older Rottweilers and, 136–37
  selecting, 53
Vitamin C, 136
Vomiting, 63
Von Gailingen bloodline, 11
Von Hohenreissach Kennel, 11
Von Stahl Kennel, 11

W–X

Walker, Herschel, 13
Water, drinking, 54, 137
Weight gain, in old Rottweilers,
  134–36
Weight pulling, 97
Wellwood Kennel, 11
Whelping, 129
  Thompson wHELPing Box,
    181–83

Y–Z

Yrüolüa, J. A. U., 5

Date Due

3.3.00			
3.31.00			

BRODART, INC.   Cat. No. 23 233   Printed in U S A